HOW TO ANALYZE PEOPLE

Learn How to Read People by Analyzing Body Language, Behavioral Psychology and Emotional Intelligence

Jenifer Thompson

© Copyright 2020 by Jenifer Thompson. All right reserved.

The work contained herein has been produced with the intent to provide relevant knowledge and information on the topic on the topic described in the title for entertainment purposes only. While the author has gone to every extent to furnish up to date and true information, no claims can be made as to its accuracy or validity as the author has made no claims to be an expert on this topic. Notwithstanding, the reader is asked to do their own research and consult any subject matter experts they deem necessary to ensure the quality and accuracy of the material presented herein.

This statement is legally binding as deemed by the Committee of Publishers Association and the American Bar Association for the territory of the United States. Other jurisdictions may apply their own legal statutes. Any reproduction, transmission, or copying of this material contained in this work without the express written consent of the copyright holder shall be deemed as a copyright violation as per the current legislation in force on the date of publishing and the subsequent time thereafter. All additional works derived from this material may be claimed by the holder of this copyright.

The data, depictions, events, descriptions and all other information forthwith are considered to be true, fair, and accurate unless the work is expressly described as a work of fiction. Regardless of the nature of this work, the Publisher is exempt from any responsibility of actions taken by the reader in conjunction with this work. The Publisher acknowledges that the reader acts of their own accord and releases the author and Publisher of any responsibility for the observance of tips, advice, counsel, strategies, and techniques that may be offered in this volume.

TABLE OF CONTENTS

Introduction 1
Chapter 1 *Why Analyze People?* 2
Chapter 2 *Get To Know Body Language* 5
Chapter 3 *Facial Expressions Speak Volumes* 9
Chapter 4 *The Fbi's Method For Eye Analysis* 12
Chapter 5 *Trust Your Intuition* 14
Chapter 6 *Become Aware Of Emotional Energy* 18
Chapter 7 *Develop Your Baseline Understanding* 22
Chapter 8 *Pay Close Attention To People Deviating Away* 26
Chapter 9 *Beware Of Cluster Gestures* 32
Chapter 10 *Compare And Contrast What You Discover* 36
Chapter 11 *Observe Mirrored Behaviors* 40
Chapter 12 *Identify The Strong Voice* 44
Chapter 13 *Pay Attention To Their Walk* 49
Chapter 14 *Be Aware Of Action Words* 53
Chapter 15 *Be Aware Of Personality Clues* 57
Chapter 16 *Never Forget To Put It Together!* 62
Chapter 17 *Make Your Guess And Validate It* 65
Chapter 18 *Be Flexible In Your Understanding* 69
Conclusion 72
Description 74

INTRODUCTION

Analyzing people is a behavior we all engage in, whether we realize it or not. In the animal kingdom, which we are all a part of, physical language is as important as verbal language. We pay attention to people's postures, body language, facial expressions, tones, and other non-verbal cues as a way to gain necessary information from people. The information we gain determines our "gut feeling" about a person, whether positive or negative and precisely what it means. Your instinct uses this as a way to determine the threats in your environment by identifying whether the threat comes from the environment itself, someone or something else, or if no threat exists at all.

Despite the fact that your primal brain is an expert with human analysis, your conscious mind may not be. In our modern lives, we have learned to ignore our instincts and follow our logic, which may not always be conditioned to pick up on the right information. For some people, their logical minds are conditioned to ignore others as a way to keep themselves comfortable and at peace in any situation.

Discovering how to analyze people consciously and intentionally is an excellent way to tap into the natural abilities of your primal brain and use them to your advantage. This analysis can allow you to determine your level of safety in an environment and help you determine how to best interact with other people. For example, you may be able to quickly identify that someone is outgoing and likes to communicate in an energized way. They may be more introverted and prefer to communicate in a more laid back manner. Knowing precisely how to engage with each person can deepen the quality of your friendships, expand your social circle, maximize your level of knowledge, and assist you with reaching your desired outcomes in any given circumstance. For example, if you are a salesperson, effective analysis can help you make better sales, or if you are a psychologist, effective analysis can help you gain deeper insight into a person's real troubles.

There are many points at which knowing how to analyze a person would be beneficial, and we are going to uncover them all and how to do it in this book. If you are ready to discover the unique skill of analyzing people, let's begin!

CHAPTER 1
Why Analyze People?

Analyzing people has many values, all of which lead to you getting what you desire out of any given situation. For example, the FBI uses analysis as a way to identify who is most likely to be guilty about something, who is lying, or who is innocent. Knowing how to adequately read people means you gain greater information from a person and a circumstance and that you can use that information to your advantage.

Another benefit of analyzing people is that it connects you with a more realistic insight into the human condition. People who do not consciously analyze other people may miss important social cues, leave themselves at risk of misunderstandings or miscommunications, or even put themselves in harmful situations due to an inability to adequately read the situation. It is important to know how to leverage this necessary primal ability so you can rely on it to support you in a number of ways, ranging from protecting you to helping you meet your desires. You will likely find your own unique reasons behind why you should learn how to analyze people. However, there are generally four core reasons behind why people analyze others': for business, social interaction, solutions, or confidence.

Analyzing People For Business

Analyzing people in business has been a necessary component of branding and marketing since the industry began. An effective analysis enables marketing experts to clearly understand the needs of their audience and meet those needs through branding and marketing initiatives. This is how they are able to design brands that match the exact desires of their audience while also creating marketing strategies that persuade their audience to interact with their brand.

Aside from creating aligned brands and marketing strategies, analysis has also enabled industries to unlock hidden growth opportunities so they can expand their businesses and industry growth. This type of analysis is often achieved by analyzing many individuals to create a large-scale analysis that represents a number of different people. In this case, they are analyzing for the majority to see what people are most interested in.

Salespeople also use analysis as a way to identify who is most likely to make a purchase and to decide how to sell to that individual. They will analyze for cues that indicate what a person cares about and what they need, then they use that to decide what to say and how to guide the experience. When they are effective, they create the exact experience their client needed to make a purchase, and they end up with a successful sale under their belts.

In business, an analysis may also be used as a way to determine which business moves a company or corporation might make. Individuals in a position of leadership or negotiation might use analysis to identify the intentions of another as they decide whether to make a business deal with that person or not. This way, they can be confident that they are making deals with honest people and getting their desires fulfilled from that deal.

Analyzing People For Social Interaction

Many people use analysis as a way to improve their social interactions. The original purpose of analysis in our primal instincts was for us to be able to determine whether someone else was a threat or not. We also used it as a way to generally analyze the tribe we were running with so that if one showed signs of distress or impending danger, the rest could be on alert and protect themselves from whatever may be threatening them. These days, the same is still useful; however, being able to analyze people can get you a lot further than threat analysis, too.

Analyzing people effectively can be a great way to make friends, grow your network, and enjoy healthier social interactions with others. When you know what to look for and how to read body language and nonverbal cues, you can quickly identify the best people to associate yourself with and the best way to engage with that individual. For example, let's say you are at a networking event, and you walk into a room filled with people that are all mingling. Through analysis, you could quickly identify the archetypes of everyone in the room so that you did not waste any time approaching people with the wrong archetype for your network. Once you identified the ones with the right archetype, you could quickly discover necessary information about how to communicate with them based on their nonverbal interactions with the room around them. From there, you could engage in a way that rapidly built your rapport, established a connection, and effectively added that person to your network.

This type of analysis is excellent for making new friends, dating new people, or just becoming better at socializing overall. Since socialization is necessary to so many areas of our lives and adds deeply to the value of our human experiences, it is well worth it to learn how to analyze people so you can enjoy improved connections with others.

Analyzing People For Solutions

Many times in life, you will be required to look for solutions to a circumstance you face. Salespeople are tasked with looking for solutions on a regular basis, as they must find solutions to meet the needs of their clients. Every day people are tasked with finding solutions to a variety of conflicts they might face, many involving other people that also need to be on board with that solution for it to work.

Analyzing people for solutions requires you to rapidly gain insight into their mood, their perspective toward the conflict, and their need. All of this can be gained by analyzing their verbal and nonverbal cues to get to the root of their concerns, at which point you can use this knowledge to propose a solution that is likely to fit that person's needs. The value of being in the position of creating and offering solutions is that you get to choose solutions that fit your needs, as well as the needs of the other person. This is an empowering position to be in, as people begin to trust in you and look toward you as the leader of that situation, which expands your reputation and the type of interactions you have with other people.

Analyzing People To Deepen Your Confidence

As social creatures, it makes sense that we thrive most when we are engaged in healthy, meaningful interactions with other people. From relationships to quick conversations at the checkout line, we value having positive interactions with others. These interactions deepen our sense of belonging, fulfillment, and satisfaction as we realize that we are accepted by others, which is a basic human need. People that learn to ignore their instinct about other people, or that have an intellectual disability that renders this instinct damaged, often lack confidence around others'. Their inability to clearly understand another often leads to them engaging in negative experiences because they cannot adequately read the situation and adjust their behavior accordingly.

Learning how to analyze people and use that analysis to make meaningful decisions about how to interact with another individual enables a person to develop greater confidence in themselves, especially when other people are concerned. Rather than feeling insecure or fearful of their interactions with others, they develop confidence in their ability to enjoy positive interactions. This increases their ability to feel as though they belong, which creates a sense of fulfillment and satisfaction on a deep, primal level.

CHAPTER 2
Get To Know Body Language

The biggest task you can tackle when it comes to discovering how to analyze other people is to learn to read body language. Much like animals in the wild communicate through their posture and movements, humans also communicate in this way. Although we rarely discuss body language as a part of everyday learning experiences, we all learn lessons of body language simply through observing others'.

Body language varies from person to person and can also have drastic differences across different cultures and groups of people. However, one can always rapidly pick up on the true intentions of another person simply through reading their body language, whether they come from the same place or not. Reading body language effectively comes partially through relying on your instinct and partially through researching the meaning of different bodily postures and cues for clearer understanding. Fortunately, psychologists and behavioral researchers have been looking into body language for years and have uncovered impressive amounts of knowledge around what the different cues mean and how they can be read.

The best way to begin reading body language is to go to a public place and start looking at different individuals. Observe their posture, physical movements, and behaviors to discover what each person is likely thinking, feeling, or doing. You will rapidly notice patterns that categorize people into different archetypes, which you can then read based on the different signs of body language below. The more you observe others' and understand what their body language means, the better you will be at reading body language as a way to analyze people.

Pay Attention To Proximity

Proximity references the amount of space between yourself and another person. When someone stands or sits close to another person, they feel a sense of closeness with that individual, which is why they have closed the space between them. If someone backs up or moves away, however, this means they are feeling uncomfortable, and they want to create more space between themselves and the other person. When a person is especially close to another individual, to the point where they are physically touching or are about to be physically touching, this indicates that they want to be physically close with that individual. This is commonly seen between romantic partners or partners that share some level of physical connection with each other.

Keep in mind that, in some cultures, it is customary to respect people's personal space, so they tend to leave more distance between themselves and others. In this case, it is helpful to pay attention to how they interact with all people and to observe their other body language indicators.

Beware Of Mirrored Behaviors

To mirror someone's behavior means to essentially mimic their behaviors. For example, if you were to stroke your hair and immediately after the person you are talking to touched their hair, this would be a sign of mimicked behaviors. Mimicked behaviors can range from posture to how you physically carry yourself or the actions you are taking, so pay close attention to how someone is mirroring someone else's behaviors. Suppose they are mirroring a lot of the behaviors. In that case, it means they are engaged with the other person and are generally interested in them. If they are not mirroring a lot of the other person's behaviors, it means they are disengaged or disinterested in that person. Be patient, though, as it can take as many as 10-30 seconds for the behavior to be mirrored by the other individual.

Look For Head Movements

Head movement can indicate a lot, such as the level of patience someone has with you or the person they are communicating with. For example, someone that nods their head slowly is interested in what you have to say and hopes you will continue talking. On the other hand, someone rapidly nodding their head means they are done listening, and they want you to stop talking so they can leave the conversation.

Aside from nodding, head tilting can indicate a lot about someone's level of interest, too. If someone tilts their head sideways while talking to another individual, this means they are interested in what the other person has to say, and they want to know more. If they tilt their head back, they are skeptical or uncertain about what the other person is saying, while tilting their head forward means they are interested or have an affinity with the speaker.

Another thing to pay attention to is the amount someone is being looked at, especially by the others around them. A person that is important and has a great rapport with others' will be looked at often, while someone who lacks significance will not be looked at by other people nearly as much. If you are looking to speak to the most powerful person in the room, look for the person that is being looked at the most.

Draw A Line From Their Toes

The direction a person's foot is facing says a lot about what they are interested in and where they truly want to be. If you are trying to analyze someone who is likely monitoring their body language and purposefully manipulating it to convey certain messages, the best thing you can do is look at their feet. Usually, people become so focused on adjusting their upper body language and facial expressions that they forget to pay attention to where their feet are directed. Their feet' direction tells you what they are interested in and what they would like to be doing at any given moment.

If a person's feet are pointed in your direction, this means that they have a favorable opinion of you and that they are interested in you. If their feet are pointed in another direction, this indicates something else. For example, feet pointed toward the door indicate someone is ready to leave, while feet pointed toward the bathroom might indicate someone needs to relieve themselves.

The next time you are in a group setting, pay attention to the directions of everyone's feet. You will quickly find out who likes who and if they are genuinely engaged with another person or not. You will also recognize who wants to leave, who would rather be elsewhere, and who is interested in continuing conversations with the person they are chatting up.

Observe Their Hand Signals

Hands also leak important information about what a person is thinking or feeling, so pay close attention to their hands and hand signals. When a person puts their hands in their pocket or on their head, this means they are either nervous or trying to deceive someone else in the room, though it can also indicate that they are relaxed depending on the rest of their body language. If their body is tense, tight, or closed off in any way, hands in the pocket indicate nervousness, while a person that is relaxed, standing with their legs apart, and seems casual, is indicating that they are comfortable in the moment.

The direction people point in or where their hands are closest to also indicates important information about that person. People will often point toward a person they have an affinity with and keep their hands generally closer to that person when they are communicating. They may not constantly point; however, you will notice they have more gestures going toward that person over anyone else, which is what indicates their level of interest.

If someone is supporting their head with their elbows on the table, this indicates they are bored. Boredom can also be witnessed in a person that stares at their hands or fidgets excessively with their hands while staring off into space. On the other hand, if they are fidgeting with their hands while rapidly looking around the room or holding a tense posture, this means they are feeling uncomfortable or nervous and are trying to relieve themselves of that energy.

Examine Their Arms

A person's arms are often considered the doorway to a person's self, as they can be used to block off the body or open it up to others. If a person stands with their arms crossed while looking at you, this typically means they are feeling defensive or intimidated by your presence. This may also indicate they are feeling vulnerable or anxious, so they want to be removed from the present moment. Alternatively, some people will cross their arms while maintaining a relaxed posture and a genuine smile, which means they are feeling relaxed and confident, though they may be trying to block off a certain aspect of themselves at that moment.

If someone places their hands on their hips, this is typically a display of dominance. Men are more likely to hold this posture than women, though women will often do it when they want to assert themselves. Some psychologists have recommended holding your hands on your hips and looking in the mirror at yourself in this posture for 60 seconds as a way to increase your self-confidence in any given moment because you see yourself holding a dominant posture. This pose indicates a deep sense of confidence and power, so you can assume anyone holding this posture feels dominant at that moment.

CHAPTER 3
Facial Expressions Speak Volumes

Facial expressions are similar to body language, except they are more subtle and fleeting than body language. Often, postures or gestures are held for at least a few seconds before changing, though they will typically last several minutes. Alternatively, facial expressions can be over within seconds, or sometimes even milliseconds, so you have to be paying close attention to catch these. Another thing about facial expressions is that you need to learn how to scan people's faces without coming across as though you are staring at them, as staring at people will completely change their mood, effectively changing their behaviors, too.

One benefit of reading facial expressions is that they tend to communicate more than the body does. While people have an easy time manipulating their body language, it can be far more challenging to monitor your facial expressions, so they do not "give you away." More often than not, people cannot control their fleeting facial expressions, which means you can rapidly gain a deeper understanding of what they think and feel, especially about particular subjects in conversation.

In general, there are seven micro expressions you can look for in a person's face, which are the fleeting expressions that indicate how they really feel. If a person is trying to save face or provide specific energy to a situation, they may try to hide these expressions in an effort to avoid having you find out what they really think or feel. Fortunately, these micro expressions happen regardless of how hard someone tries to avoid it, so if you watch for them, you will certainly see them.

Expressions Of Surprise

Expressions of surprise can be seen in a person raising their eyebrows to the point where they curve, and the skin below the eyebrow stretches out. You will also see horizontal wrinkles across the forehead, as their brows press up far enough to allow their eyelids to open more than is typical, too. Often, a person that is surprised will have their jaw drop open, and their teeth will be parted, though there should be no tension or stretching of the mouth itself. In the dating world, when someone gives you a fleeting look of surprise, this is said to be a good sign that they are attracted to you, interested in you, and that they want to spend more time with you.

Expressions Of Fear

Fear can be seen in the eyebrows as well, as they will be raised though they will also be drawn together, creating a flat line across the brows. You will see wrinkles on the forehead, but they are at the center of it between the person's eyebrows only. Often, their upper eyelid will be raised, but the lower eyelid will be drawn up as it has become tenser. Often, you will see a lot of white above the iris of the eye, but no white below the iris, because of how far the eyes are drawn up. In the mouth area, their mouth will be open with their lips slightly tensed or stretched. Some people may also draw their lips back, making a dimple in the sides of their mouths.

Expressions Of Disgust

Disgust can be seen in the face whenever a person narrows their eyes, raises their upper lip and cheeks, and wrinkles their nose. In some cases, their upper lip may be raised so high that you can see their upper teeth, too. Disgust is not only a reaction to seeing or smelling something gross; it can also be toward something a person hears about. For example, if you are out with a new friend and you say something they are disgusted by, such as mentioning a food you like that they don't, you might see this expression on their face.

Expressions Of Anger

Anger is often easy to witness in someone's face, though some people will attempt to hide their anger, which means you need to pay close attention to their faces. When a person is angry, their eyebrows will be lowered and drawn together, creating vertical lines at the center of their forehead, between their eyebrows. Their lower lip will be tensed in a pout-like position, and their lips may be firmly pressed together with the corners of the mouth drawn down and their lower jaw jutting out. Often, their eyes will be glaring or even bulging because they are so angry. You might also notice that their nostrils are flaring.

Expressions Of Happiness

When a person is happy, their face looks soft and drawn back. Even if they are not smiling, the corners of their mouth are often drawn back and up, and they may even have their mouth parted with their teeth exposed. Often, a wrinkle will run from the outer nostril to the outer corner of the lip, indicating they are feeling happy. When a person smiles, even subtly, their cheeks will be raised, and their lower eyelid might have small wrinkles or tension. Crow's feet near the outside of the eyes also indicates that a person is feeling happy at that moment. The more defined the various wrinkles and lines of happiness are, the happier someone is feeling.

Expressions Of Sadness

When a person is sad, the inner corners of their eyebrows will be drawn in and up, creating either a flat brow or a brow that arches down toward the edges of the face. Below their eyebrows, the skin may be triangulated with the inner corner up. Often, the corners of their lips will be drawn down, but their jaw will be drawn up. Their lower lip will also pout, though it may be subtle in some people, especially if they are trying to hide their sadness from others.

Expressions Of Contempt Or Hate

The only way to really recognize a look of contempt or hate is to look for someone that has one side of the mouth raised, despite the rest of the face being neutral or natural. Contempt and hate indicate someone is feeling negative toward another individual or something that an individual is saying. This is the only microexpression that is asymmetrical, as all of the other ones are symmetrical in nature.

CHAPTER 4
The Fbi's Method For Eye Analysis

Studies have shown that eye movement indicates what is going on in someone's brain, and therefore what they are likely feeling or thinking in any given moment. Paying close attention to someone's eye movement allows you to recognize whether they are truthful or not at any given moment. The most important things to notice are where a person is looking and what they are specifically doing with their eyes. Generally, the eyes are used as a way to identify dishonesty in someone, as there are common indicators people use that express their dishonesty through their eyes. However, if you do not see these indicators, chances are you are talking to a person that is telling you the truth.

Pay Attention To Where Their Eyes Go

Where someone spends most of their time looking reveals a lot about what they are thinking or feeling. When a person frequently looks at you and pays close attention to what you are doing, this indicates that they are interested in you and want to know more about you. If a person looks excessively at someone else, this means they are more interested in that individual, and they want to know more about them. A person who stares heavily at a specific object or place is revealing what they would rather be doing. For example, if a person stares heavily toward the door, they want to leave, while a person that stares heavily toward a television would rather be watching TV than doing whatever they are presently doing. People look at what they are interested in or at the person or object that has their attention most.

Eye Signals Of Lying

If a person is lying, their eyes will move up and to the right because they are attempting to make something up on the spot or recall the lie they made up previously. If, however, a person looks up and to the left, they are likely telling the truth because the way they are looking indicates they are trying to remember a real piece of information. If someone is looking around, it may not necessarily mean they are lying, though. Some people will move their eyes a lot to process information, which is an entirely different movement.

Eye Signals Of Stress

If someone is feeling stressed, you will see it through increased blinking. The average person blinks between 8 to 21 times per minute, so if someone is blinking excessively, such as once every two or three seconds, this means they are stressed out by the present moment. They may be stressed overall, or they may be feeling pressured to answer a question properly, which introduces temporary stress to their system.

Eye Signals Of Disgust / Distaste

When someone feels disgusted with something, they will often narrow their eyes. The more narrow someone's eyes are, the more disgusted they are feeling at that moment, so be aware of *how* narrow their eyes are to better understand how they are feeling.

Eye Signals Of Discomfort

When someone is uncomfortable, they will do something called "eye blocking." Eye blocking means they are trying to cover their eyes to avoid you seeing them. If they cannot reasonably block their eyes, they may avoid eye contact altogether in an effort to avoid having to make eye contact when they are uncomfortable.

Eye Signals Of Happiness

When a person is feeling happy, their eyes may do many things. Often, they will arch their eyebrows and smile. They will also have enlarged pupils, which is a sign that you like something. In fact, studies have shown that if you look at someone or something you love, your pupil size will automatically increase, indicating your affection. Of course, this may not be easy to witness in other people, but you might be able to see it if you pay close enough attention.

Eye Signals Of Fear Or Surprise

If a person is feeling fearful or surprised, their eyes will often be wide open. They might also have a fleeting look of surprise where their eyes go from wide to wider and back to wide, indicating that they are especially surprised by something. This is an automatic response caused by adrenaline in the body, which you can witness in someone else if you pay close enough attention.

Eye Signals Of Focus

When someone is especially focused, their pupils will usually constrict, and their eyes will remain fixated on what has their focus. However, if they are focused on something that is in the distance, their pupils will actually dilate instead.

CHAPTER 5
Trust Your Intuition

Your intuition, or instinct, knows more than you think. This inner compass is fixed to the primal part of your brain, and it knows how to pick up information from a situation that your conscious self may not have picked up on otherwise. While we are often conditioned to ignore this part of ourselves, we can learn to regain a connection with it by trusting our intuition and using it regularly.

Psychologists and researchers believe our intuitions and instincts are so powerful because they are reading information that our conscious mind does not have time for. In one second, you process more than 11,000,000 pieces of information. Naturally, your conscious mind does not have time to sort through all of that information to decipher what it all means, so it focuses instead on what is relevant to you at that moment. In other words, it fixates on what you have chosen to bring into your conscious awareness. Just because you are not consciously thinking about all of these things does not mean they cease to exist, however. Your brain is still taking in all of this information, and your subconscious mind is still sorting through it all to better understand what it all means. If it finds something of importance, it raises it up through your awareness of the necessary level of consciousness. If it does not feel the need to raise it to your conscious awareness or does not have a complete set of information to raise to your conscious awareness, it will feed it into your intuition or instinct instead. Thus, you get those "gut feelings" about different circumstances, places, things, and *people*.

Don't Overthink Your Intuition

Your intuition is said to be a fast judge of character, and it is often more accurate than your logical mind, too. However, if you overthink your intuition or any of the information you have perceived through your intuition, you will disrupt your results and find yourself experiencing inaccuracies. The best way to analyze a person with your intuition is to trust the first gut feeling you get about them, or the feeling you get based on their first impression.

If you are observing someone to better understand their body language, facial expressions, tone, or even the meaning of their words, pay close attention to the initial reaction you have to whatever they have said. You will immediately pick up on whether or not they are trustworthy, what emotions are behind their words, and what thoughts they likely have that drive their emotion.

Avoid Attaching To Intuitive Beliefs

Intuition can provide you an excellent insight into a given situation; however, it is not helpful to attach yourself to your intuitive beliefs, especially if new information is presented. For example, if you believe someone wants to do something with you based on your intuition, but they verbally express that they do not want to, it is unhelpful to attach to the belief that they do want to and that they must be lying if they said otherwise. Attaching to beliefs is unhealthy, can remove you from reality, and can lead to uncomfortable or unfair situations between yourself and another individual.

One way that people tend to rapidly attach to their intuitive beliefs is through their dreams. When a person dreams of something, they can attach to the idea that their dreams are true and might refuse to believe anything that states otherwise. For example, if a person was planning on going on vacation but dreams about a plane crash, they might cancel the vacation or experience excess stress on the plane because of their dream. In this case, they have attached to the idea that their dream was real, and their intuition was warning them against the vacation, despite the fact that this was not something rooted in logic, reasoning, or facts.

Another way people tend to do this with others is by believing in something completely untrue and then developing anxiety over it. For example, you might have an intuitive feeling that someone is harshly judging you, and that feeling causes you to feel anxious and scared. You might even try to change yourself or twist yourself to conform to their beliefs because you want them to change their opinion. If, however, they are not actually harshly judging you and you have misinterpreted their signals, you are wasting your time and maybe causing an uncomfortable social experience in the process. It helps to listen to your intuition *and* trust that people will tell you the truth about what they are thinking and feeling. Even if they are not, it is not your responsibility to force someone to express their genuine judgments. Respect their right to stay quiet, and focus on yourself.

Practice Improves Your Intuition

Like anything, your intuition can be improved upon with practice. To improve your intuition, you simply need to listen to it more and trust the feelings it gives you. For example, if you are in a room and your intuition tells you that the room is dangerous or that you should leave it, trust it and leave that space. You might not understand why, and the reasoning may never be revealed to you, but so long as you trust your intuition, you are reinforcing it and encouraging it to continue supporting your wellbeing.

Another way you can improve your intuition, which can directly help you analyze people, is through quieting your mind and giving your intuition space to work. If you are continually thinking back through everything you logically and reasonably know, you will be dominating your mind with thoughts that drown your intuition out. Try clearing your mind, observing another person, and inviting your intuition to provide you with feedback on that other individual. Then, read that feedback to get a clearer understanding of what your intuition is telling you.

Insight Is Seeing, Intuition Is Sensing

It is important to recognize that your insight and intuition are two separate things. Insight suggests you have actually seen something, such as the way a person is behaving or knowledge that allows you to better understand the way a person is behaving. Intuition, on the other hand, allows you to sense what another person is thinking or feeling. You might be able to sense information behind their behaviors, or that indicate why they are engaging in specific behaviors. However, intuition is only a feeling or a gut reaction; it is not a guarantee.

In order to effectively use your intuition in things such as analyzing people, it is helpful to allow your intuition to draw you to a conclusion, then use your logic and reasoning to determine whether your conclusion is accurate or not. If your insight suggests you misinterpreted that person, you might use your intuition to gain further knowledge based on what you learned through insight, but you should never assume that your insight is wrong. Always trust your intuition to guide you, but be willing to look for more information to guarantee your findings.

Stress Favors Intuition

When you are in a stressful situation, your intuition will tell you everything you need to know to navigate that experience. Intuition is spectacular at helping you move through troubling experiences effectively, so you remain safe throughout that experience. If you are in a situation where you are stressed out, and your intuition starts telling you something about the people around you, you can generally trust your intuition to be a fairly good judge of character.

However, if you are feeling sad, your intuition is not nearly as strong. When you are sad, your intuition is likely to be drowned out by a voice in your head that makes you feel worse. That voice will attempt to convince you that it is your intuition, but it isn't. As it attempts to convince you, it will also try to tell you that everything is bad, things are going wrong, no one likes you, and there is no hope for you. You can tell this is not your intuition because it speaks messages of hopelessness and defeat, rather than clear signals of how to get yourself out of that situation.

Be careful not to rely on your intuition when you are feeling sad or depressed, as doing so could lead to you trusting false information and struggling to truly read the other person. Instead, rely on more practical measures such as reading their body language, facial expressions, and eyes.

You Can Read People Through Their Writing

One fascinating way that you can read people through your intuition is by reading them through their writing. In this day and age, everyone is on social media writing about what they are doing, how they are feeling, or what they are thinking about. Fascinatingly, you can read what someone has written and gained insight into who they are and what they are experiencing based on their words. Similarly to witnessing darting eyes, a tense brow, pressed lips or raised cheeks, you can read someone based on the words they use, their punctuation and grammar, and the general tone of their messages.

When a person writes emails, social media posts, streams of consciousness, blog posts, or anything else online, they are using cues that indicate who they are and what they are communicating. An excellent cue to look for would be the language they are using. People that swear, especially frequently, communicate that they are likely highly neurotic, lack conscientiousness, and are unlikely to be agreeable with others. If they use any words that suggest anger, the same can generally be assumed. When a person speaks in the past tense, this is likely to indicate that they are depressed, while words like "know" in a diary suggest that they are feeling depressed, also.

Another way you can judge someone's character online is by looking at their profile. What username are they using? What is their profile picture? How have they described themselves in their bio? You can tell if someone is fun, whimsical, professional, angry, judgmental, self-centered, flamboyant, incompetent, or friendly based on how they have designed their profile and what words they have chosen to use.

A great way to practice using your intuition to help you identify someone's character is to look at people's social media profiles. Spend time analyzing profiles to get a feel for what type of personality someone has. Scan over their entire profile and trust your intuition to guide you to the right conclusion on who that person likely is. Then, if possible, scroll their posts and see if they align with the assumption you have drawn.

CHAPTER 6
Become Aware Of Emotional Energy

Emotional energy is a form of energy that we all carry, and it is expressed through our verbal and nonverbal cues. Everyone can sense and experience emotional energy because it is a commonly used form of communication that allows humans to share important information with each other. From person to person, emotional communication can help people connect or ward off the other person. In groups, emotional communication can help the rest of the group become aware of a problem or increase their feelings of comfort and relaxation, depending on what is going on.

Like with all other forms of analysis, you can read energy through your intuition. However, there are other ways to read emotional energy, too. Learning how to read emotional energy practically ensures that you will have the ability to rely on your intuition and your knowledge to effectively read a person. This way, you gain more accurate reading, and you can use that knowledge to your benefit.

Sense People's Presence

People emit energy when they are present in a space, and that energy can be felt by everyone else. An excellent way to recognize this fact is to consider the last time a friend visited your house; you could feel their energy in your home. It is easy to sense someone else's energy in your home because this is a place where you spend a lot of time, so when the energy changes, it is noticeable. Another excellent way to sense people's presence is to think about the different energies between someone, such as the Dalai Lama versus Charles Manson.

Everyone, including yourself, exudes certain energy when they are present, and it pays to identify what that energy is anytime you meet someone new. Pay close attention to the overall energy people emit and the way it makes you feel. Notice when they feel warm, positive, and enjoyable to be around, or when they feel cold, detached, or draining to be around. These all indicate specific energy archetypes that the person is likely to have.

Pay Attention To Their Eyes

The age-old saying "Eyes are the window to a person's soul" is true. You can express love, hate, and many other powerful emotions through your eyes. Science has shown that your brain emits electromagnetic signals through the eyes that can be sensed by other people, and vice versa. You can sense this energy anytime you feel someone staring at you, even if you were not originally looking at that person.

If you want to know what emotions a person is feeling, look into their eyes, and pay close attention to the types of looks they give back. Trust your intuition, but be aware of other tell-tale signs, too. If they refuse to look at you, they may be uncomfortable or angry with you or with something else that is causing them to feel disconnected from others'. If they look deep into your eyes and you feel seen, received, and loved, you know they have an energy of compassion and empathy. If you feel hated, uncomfortable, or like you are being hunted, you are in the presence of someone that does not have your best interest at heart. Your intuition will tell you the true meaning behind someone's glance, so trust that and incorporate it into your overall analysis to get a clear image of how a person is feeling and what they are thinking.

Feel Their Physical Touches

A person's physical touches heavily communicate the way they are feeling. The primary points of touch include handshakes, hugging, random touching, and welcomed touching. Each of these touch-based experiences can communicate significant amounts of energy to you, so pay attention.

Handshakes are a form of touch that you can experience with anyone, and you can initiate with anyone at appropriate times, too. You can gain a significant amount of information from a handshake, as this simple form of touch can tell you if a person is feeling weak or confident, engaged or disinterested, outgoing or withdrawn. How a person's body language is surrounding that handshake says a lot, too. If a person leans toward you, is fully facing you, looks at you, or has their feet pointed toward you, they are engaged and feeling good about your conversation. If they are neutral or holding themselves back in any way, they are not interested in communicating at that moment.

Hugs can say a lot, too. If a person hugs you from the side or pats your back during a hug, this indicates they feel friendly toward you but not as though you are super close. The pat indicates the person is feeling uneasy, and while they care about you, they are uncertain as to what the appropriate form of expression is to convey that. If a person hugs you from behind, this means they see you as a lover; it is only ever shared between lovers, too. Hugs from behind indicate a person feels protective over you, and they want to show you how much they cherish you through this hug. When a person offers you a tight hug, especially when that hug turns into an embrace, it means they are letting you know they care. A-frame hugs are hugs where a person hugs you out of obligation, not desire, so they keep most of their body away from you except for their shoulders.

Random acts of touching are acts that are not necessary nor expected, but they do happen. For example, if someone touches your shoulder, arm, or leg when you are talking to them. Touching is almost never accidental, as we tend to be highly aware of who we are around and will avoid touching or physically connecting with someone if we truly do not want to. If someone is making contact with you, it is because they want to. This virtually always signals that the person is interested in you and engaged at that moment. In some cases, these touches indicate a person cares or is connecting with you to help you feel better. If it seems random to you, however, it is likely that they are communicating interest in you.

Intentional acts of touching are most common among lovers, and they can say a lot. Since you likely experience touch from your partner often, you can tell a change in their emotions based on a change in their touch. Less touching, lighter touching, or seemingly restrictive touching indicates that a person is feeling disconnected or like they do not actually want to be in physical contact at that moment. If your partner does this, they may be feeling stressed out, having a hard day, or struggling with a sense of disconnect between the two of you. If your partner is touching you more than usual, this indicates they want to feel closer to you, so they are trying to get closer to your physical space. You can always ask them to communicate their thoughts, feelings, and needs if you require clarification on why they are behaving the way they are.

Listen To Their Tone And Laugh

You can immediately tell if someone is fake in their communication or laughter, based exclusively on their tones. A person with a tone and laugh that is genuine will come from a deep, centered place, and their voice and laughter will sound hearty and full. If they sound hollow, empty, or forced, they are faking it to cover up what they are really feeling or thinking.

You can also hear emotions such as anger, sadness, low confidence, anxiety, insensitivity, and arrogance in a person's voice. Simply through listening to their tone and the way they are enunciating their words, you can pick up on the different emotions in their voice. This particular form of hearing is best achieved by listening to many emotions, which allows you to genuinely hear the differences in emotion. Often, they are so subtle that attempting to explain them would be challenging. A great way to practice hearing emotional energy in a person's voice is to listen to videos or recordings with people that have many different emotions. See if you can identify each emotion as it surfaces, and then check to see if your assumption was correct. This way, you can start to pick up on hearing emotional energy in people's voices and laughs.

Sense Their Heart Energy

Each of us has heart energy that we can bring, or leave, from any experience. When a person brings their heart energy, you feel a sense of fullness around that person. They communicate and behave in ways that make it clear that they have shown up as their full selves and that they feel deeply invested in the present moment. If a person does not bring their heart energy, you can sense that, too, as they seem to be lacking a certain "something." Often, a person that is guarding their heart or purposefully leaving it out of a situation emanates an energy that is ineffable or difficult to describe. Something about them just feels "off" or "missing." If you know a person well, you will be able to quickly tell if their heart is not in it, while people you have just met may require more patience as you learn how to read their unique energy and expressions.

With some people, you can just tell that they are not fully invested in what they are doing or saying. With others, you need to pay closer attention. Can you feel their warmth, unconditional love, and positive intentions radiating as they move through life? Or does it seem like they are agitated, annoyed, or frustrated with the things they have been tasked with? People with big heart energy will always express some form of passion and peace, even if they are doing something they dislike because, at their core, they are a genuinely passionate and peaceful person. Those that completely lack these expressions during times of stress or disappointment are disconnected from their heart and may not be behaving or communicating authentically at that moment. If they are generally disconnected from their heart, they may not know how to behave or communicate authentically at all. In this case, you need to pay more attention to their expressions and nonverbal language so you can get a clearer interpretation of their real intentions and messages.

CHAPTER 7
Develop Your Baseline Understanding

Armed with the knowledge you have, you are ready to start analyzing people. It is not helpful, however, to go into the process with a variety of knowledge and no palpable way to apply that knowledge in the actual moment. When you are actively analyzing people, you do not have time to pause, read through your book, identify their behavior, and move on to the next one. Body language, facial expressions, eyes, and emotional energy are expressed and changed so rapidly that it would be impossible for you to read everything step by step. That is why, in effective human analysis, there is a process you can follow that allows you to effortlessly read someone, gain accurate feedback, and move on to the next portion of your reading. This process starts with creating your baseline analysis. A baseline analysis will vary depending on the situation you are in. With people that you know well or are around frequently, you have many encounters to generate baseline data, so you know how they generally behave. For people that you will only see once or twice, you do not have nearly as much time to put together an understanding of how that person generally behaves or what their overall baseline is. Instead, you will put one together that is relevant to your interaction and use that to define the rest of your analysis.

The Meaning Of A Baseline

A person's baseline is their typical behavior. This defines the average emotional state of an individual, as well as their typical thoughts, actions, perspectives, and their overall approach to life. Baselines can easily be summarized in a few words or less, which makes defining and tracking them easier.

The purpose of a baseline analysis is that it allows you to understand what their average behavior is like, which allows you to identify when they have deviated away from that baseline. For example, let's say your boss is generally a hard ruler. Perhaps he tends to deliver orders with a harsh tone, has high expectations, and is not afraid to ream someone out if they fail to meet those expectations fully. This would be your boss's baseline analysis. If one day, your boss came to work and was not doling out consequences, snapping orders at people, and ruling with a hard fist, you would know something was off.

Baselines are important because they help you understand how your actions, others' actions, or the circumstances are affecting a person. You may need to have this awareness so you can take actions that support someone, protect yourself, or resolve the conflict of a situation you might face. In some cases, baselines will be unimportant because your analysis will not require further action, but there will be many times in your life that you have to communicate with others, and using baselines is an excellent way to gauge your effectiveness.

Baselines In Long Term Relationships

In long term relationships, you have a significant number of opportunities to identify someone's baseline and build on it. People's long term baseline changes over time, so your general understanding of a person is likely to change over time, too. For example, your friend might have been a carefree, spontaneous type of person, then they had a child, and now they are more reserved and careful. These types of changes, especially in response to life experiences, are entirely normal. The benefit of knowing a person's long term baseline is that you can become aware of how they have changed, and you can learn a lot about them through those changes. You also discover how you can better interact with them based on these changes and continue to enjoy an excellent relationship with them.

The baseline in a long term relationship will start off the same as a baseline in a one-off encounter because when you first meet someone, you do not have any historical data to add to your baseline analysis. As you continue to get to know them, you gain significant insight into how they tend to think, feel, and behave in different situations, which allows you to build a more dynamic baseline.

The more you learn about a person and their baseline in different situations, the more you understand them. This understanding may be seemingly irrelevant, or it may help you connect with or support the people in your life better. For example, let's say you have a friend that is generally optimistic and outgoing in all areas of her life, but when it comes to her career, she seems more intimidated and shy and behaves completely differently. This lets you know that something in her career is causing her to feel a lack of confidence. You may or may not be in a position to support her; however, this awareness allows you to have greater compassion and empathy for the experiences she has in this part of her life.

You will come to discover people's baselines so long as they are a long-term fixture in your life, whether you intend to or not. For example, your family, friends, coworkers, and other people you see on a regular basis will all become people with whom you share long term relationships. Knowing the baselines of people in these long term relationships allows you to use this to your advantage anytime you need to, which can be a powerful position to hold at any given time in your life.

Baselines In One-Off Encounters

In one-off encounters, you do not have nearly as much time to create a baseline, which means you must accept that right from the start, your baseline analysis will be incomplete. With people such as the person that serves you coffee, a person you are selling something to, or a person on the bus, you do not have insight into how they tend to behave in their everyday life. You lack awareness around their baseline with their family, work, friends, hobbies, and in other key areas of their lives where they are likely to express their true baseline personality. The trouble with this is that you only have so much to go from, which means you only know their baseline at that moment. However, for most short term encounters, that is all you need.

Let's say you are working retail, and someone comes into your store angry because of an experience they had with the company you are working for. To you, their baseline is angry because this is the only way you have seen them. Although this is unlikely to be their overall baseline, it is the baseline you can analyze and use to help you assess how well or not your conversation is going. If, after talking with them, they deviate toward anger, you know your actions are not supporting their situation. If, however, they start to deviate toward more peaceful and cheerful, you know that your solution is fulfilling their need and they are satisfied with their experience.

In many one-off encounters, you will not directly engage with the person whose baseline you are reading. However, you may want to know their baseline so you can observe how they deviate from it in encounters with other people. This information may not be directly relevant to you, but it can help you gain a deeper understanding of how people tend to behave, what may affect their baseline, and what to look for when reading people. The more you practice reading people, even if you are not directly associated with that person, the better you will get at this skill.

Defining Someone's Baseline

The actual act of defining someone's baseline should be done immediately upon meeting someone, before ever trying to understand what their verbal or nonverbal communications mean about that specific moment. To identify someone's baseline, give yourself about 1-2 minutes to observe the way they carry themselves and make a conclusion from what you discover. You will create your baseline from their body language, facial expressions, eye movements, and overall energy.

Once you have established their baseline, give yourself another 3-5 minutes to confirm that your conclusion is correct, and to judge how flexible they are with their baseline. If they are particularly flexible, they will rapidly deviate away from your initial conclusion. If they are not, they will remain consistent in their baseline.

If someone's baseline is something you find pleasant or that you want to continue experiencing, pay close attention to the thing that causes their baseline to change and elect to encourage circumstances that maintain or improve their baseline. If you want their baseline to change, such as if they are in a low mood, beware of behaviors that change their circumstances, and engage only in those that improve the way they are feeling.

Anytime you are directly engaging with someone, you always want to pay attention to how your behavior affects their baseline and adjust your behavior to affect their baseline in a positive, not negative, way. It is important, however, not to use this as a way to fuel people-pleasing behaviors. Your goal is not to betray yourself or your needs to fulfill someone else's so that they are happy. Instead, you must remain consistent in having your needs fulfilled, though you can go about getting them fulfilled in a way that aligns with the other person, too. The real goal is to use their baseline and the behaviors that cause them to deviate as a way to understand how you can get your needs met through that person if the circumstances warrant it. Otherwise, this is merely for observational and educational purposes.

CHAPTER 8
Pay Close Attention To People Deviating Away

Deviations define the process of someone moving away from their baseline personality. Generally, deviations can be positive, negative, or neutral. When a person deviates away from their baseline, this indicates that something has caused them to feel different from their normal state. Every person deviates from their baseline, so this is entirely normal behavior. However, deviations can tell you a lot about a person overall, as well as in that present moment.

As you learn to analyze people, it is helpful to pay attention to when and where deviations occur, as well as what is causing them. In some cases, observing deviations will merely support your ability to create a deeper understanding of humans and their tendencies. In other cases, deviations allow you to understand how you or your environment is influencing someone and possibly provide you with opportunities to use that to your advantage.

It is important to realize that observing specific behaviors from people does not mean you are required to act on that information. For the most part, recognizing these behaviors will not require any effort on your behalf; it will merely serve as added data for you to monitor, which will assist you in future endeavors. When it does come time for you to act on that data, however, deviations serve as a key opportunity for you to determine the best course of action for you to take, should you have needs that require fulfillment.

People Routinely Deviate From Their Baseline

Firstly, you must understand that people routinely deviate from their baseline. When you are with people for an incredibly short period of time, you may witness only one or two deviations, or you may not witness any. As you spend more time with people, however, you will witness significant deviations from their baseline as people are constantly being affected by their environment, the people around them, and even the experiences they have within themselves.

Deviations from baselines may be spontaneous, or they may be habitual. Spontaneous deviations indicate a person is experiencing an unusual reaction to something which has drawn them away from their baseline. An excellent example would be if a person had recently experienced a tragedy such as a car accident or a sudden loss, which would cause a deviation. These types of deviations can be significant and can elicit unusual behavior from an individual. These unusual behaviors are generally more challenging to analyze and predict unless you are accustomed to analyzing people across many situations.

Habitual deviations are routinely experienced and generally occur on a daily, weekly, or monthly basis. They are common, to the point where even you experience these deviations on a regular basis. Habitual deviations are caused by triggers which a person is routinely exposed to, thus causing them to deviate from their baseline to fulfill that habitual experience. These deviations are triggered by common occurrences in one's life, such as career, family, friends, hobbies, specific songs or TV shows, or other experiences. For example, a person that is generally calm and friendly might become competitive and assertive when faced with their career because this persona suits their career better.

Habitual deviations are experienced in virtually every area of someone's life and can be defined as categorical baselines, or baselines that are relevant to each area of a person's life. If you were to observe someone's categorical baselines, you would quickly recognize that they had baselines specific to eight areas of their lives: health, wealth, career, relationships, love, hobbies, their relationship with themselves, and their faith. Each of these areas can cause a person to experience different feelings, thoughts, and behaviors. If you have people that are close to you in your life, you can likely reflect on them or observe them and immediately witness these changed baselines. Overall, however, the baselines should all work together to create that individuals' primary baseline, or the baseline that represents who they are as a whole individual.

Negative Deviations Indicate Something Is Wrong

Negative deviations are those that cause an individual to experience negative emotions or engage in negative behaviors. Often, their thoughts and perspectives will follow a pessimistic suit, too. If a person experiences negative deviations from their baseline, you can easily assume something is likely wrong in that person's world. Negative deviations themselves will not tell you what is wrong, but they will indicate that said person is experiencing frustrations or challenges in a key area of their life.

The four likely influences of negative deviations are self, environment, others, and circumstances. Each of these can cause a person to experience a negative mood, thoughts, feelings, or behaviors. You must analyze their other cues to identify which is the likely cause of their negative deviation.

If a person is experiencing a negative deviation caused by themselves, they are being challenged by self-limiting beliefs, low confidence or self-esteem, or thoughts that are causing them to feel bad about themselves. People commonly dig into negative memories that were recalled based on a recent trigger, which causes them to experience a negative deviation.

For example, if a person was routinely bullied about something as a child, anytime they faced that trigger as an adult, they may have a negative deviation because they recall these painful memories.

If a person experiences negative deviation because of their environment, they are struggling to thrive within that space. The triggers they experience are caused by the space around them, and they cause that person to feel as though they cannot be happy or content within that space. Some triggers may be fleeting, such as a messy kitchen or laundry on the floor, while others may be more persistent. For example, some people are triggered by their place of employment because it has caused so much stress for them.

If a person experiences negative deviation due to others, they have been negatively impacted by another individual in one way or another. This can happen following conflict, betrayal, disappointment, unfulfilled expectations, or other challenges one may face with another individual. These negative deviations may be relieved once the conflict has been resolved, or it may be relieved once the offending individual leaves that person's space.

If a person experiences negative deviations caused by their circumstances, they are likely to deviate away from their baseline in all areas of their lives. Circumstances like trauma, major conflict, unexpected life changes, or situations that cause failure to thrive can all negatively affect a person. When they experience these negative deviations, they are only healed once that person's circumstances improve. They are often capable of adjusting the circumstances themselves, though some take time to be fully adjusted.

Positive Deviations Indicate Someone Is Pleased

Positive deviations are those that cause an individual to experience something positive or pleasant in relation to their baseline. Even people that have a generally positive baseline can experience positive deviations as they move from happiness or gratitude to excitement or elation. When a person experiences a positive deviation, this means something excellent is happening in their world that is promoting this positive experience.

Like with negative deviations, positive deviations are caused by one's self, environment, others, or their circumstances. You must observe a person's overall cues to gain more insight into what has encouraged a positive mood. With positive deviations, these can be particularly helpful with building relationships or positively impacting someone's life as you gain insight into what enables them to have these positive deviations. For example, if you learn that your friend is especially excited by surprises, you can plan surprises for them as a way to promote a positive deviation from their baseline anytime you want to celebrate them or help them enjoy the most out of life.

Positive deviations stimulated by one's self are the most powerful form of positive deviations. A person that can stimulate this deviation on their own knows how to elevate themselves out of a low place, which means they can improve their wellbeing without the necessary assistance of anyone else. Their positive deviations can be caused by experiences they created for themselves, their thoughts, beliefs, or values.

Positive deviations stimulated by one's environment indicate that they feel in their element in that environment, which causes them to thrive. When a person thrives in a given environment, they are more likely to experience improved mood, greater resiliency, increased determination, and a significant will to achieve anything they set out to achieve. Often, they experience a boost to their self-confidence and self-esteem, too, which is excellent for one's well being.

Positive deviations caused by other people are a wonderful sign that someone is pleased by another person's presence. Positive deviations in social settings can be caused by surrounding ourselves with people we like or sharing pleasant experiences with people we enjoy. If you are engaged in analyzing a person, and you want to have a positive impact on that individual, sharing pleasant experiences with them is a wonderful way to have a better experience with that person.

Positive deviations caused by one's circumstances means that someone is likely celebrating something meaningful in their life. A new birth, a promotion, a scholarship, engagements, new opportunities, and other experiences can all stimulate one to experience a positive deviation from their baseline.

As with negative deviations, most positive deviations are short-lived, though they will have a significant impact on someone's wellbeing. Generally, people that experience more positive deviations will enjoy greater health, improved self-confidence and self-esteem, and more fulfillment from life because they experience positive things on a regular basis.

Behaviors, Circumstances, And Experiences Affect Deviations

Every baseline can be affected by behaviors, circumstances, and experiences. While each person is responsible for their own baseline, it is common for other people's behaviors, circumstances, and experiences to impact another's baseline, too. People that are generally more resilient, leadership-oriented, and persistent in life tend to have greater control over their baseline, which allows them to refrain from being affected unnecessarily by things in their lives. This does not mean that a person will not have negative or positive deviations; those are inevitable and are experienced by everyone. However, people with greater control will generally experience fewer deviations, or more intentional deviations, because they are less affected by the people around them.

It is important to recognize the level to which a person is affected by the world around them if you want to observe more about who they are and how they are influenced. People that are easily affected by external factors can be easy to manipulate and affect and can also be more flighty and lack commitment. You must be continually influencing this individual to remain on the same page as you if you are attempting to work with someone that is routinely affected by external influences; otherwise, you can quickly lose them. If you are not carefully managing them, you may not be able to rely on them whatsoever as they let someone or something else talk them out of maintaining their commitment with you or anyone else.

If you are talking to someone that experiences lesser influences from the outside world, you can safely assume that they are a more controlled, logical, and poised individual. These individuals tend to be excellent leaders, critical thinkers, and intentional in their actions because they know how to win at the game of life. As such, once they make an observation, they generally stick to their original belief because they feel confident in their process. If you can successfully motivate someone like this to get on your team or commit to something with you, you can feel confident that they will remain committed because they take their commitment seriously.

The more someone expresses this level of self-control, the more you need to be intentional about how you interact with them if you ever need to gain something from that person. People with greater self-control are typically knowledgeable in human behavior and engage in analysis themselves on a consistent basis, which means they will be watching you as closely as you are watching them. Being intentional and careful, as well as authentic and full-spirited, ensures your ability to interact with that person in a way they will be positively receptive toward.

It Is Not Your Job To People Please

One thing you have to be cautious with when it comes to analyzing people, especially if you intend to use that analysis to direct your behaviors, is people-pleasing. People pleasers are individuals that read people's baseline and deviations and use that information to manipulate themselves in a way that is intended to make the other person happy. This is rarely done with their own wellbeing in mind; rather, they are focused solely on the wellbeing of the other person. In the end, that person ends up running themselves thin and abandoning themselves and their own needs in favor of everyone else's. You never want to do that to yourself.

It is not your job to people-please. Learning to analyze people is not a step toward people-pleasing; rather, it is a step away from people-pleasing. When you learn to adequately analyze people, you no longer have to assume that it is your responsibility to make them happy because it never was in the first place. Instead, you can understand what they require to reach certain points and offer them guidance to get to that place. This means you end up having your own needs met while effectively collaborating with someone else and their natural personality to get their needs met.

An excellent example of using analysis as a way to avoid people-pleasing, rather than encourage it, would be in a place of business. Let's say you are a manager and you need to pitch your boss on something that would make work much easier for your team; however, your boss does not tend to be the type of person that likes to make changes to the system. If you knew how to analyze him, you could read his behaviors, identify what causes positive deviation, and use that to your advantage so you can encourage him to be in a positive deviation when you ask for the change to be implemented. Chances are, you can get him to "yes" a lot easier this way. The same can be done when it comes to getting any of your wants or needs met, though you should be careful to only ever use this when it creates a positive outcome for everyone if you attempt to manipulate the situation, so your needs are met but no one else's, you will find yourself engaged in negative manipulation, which can be dangerous to yourself and others. This can also create a negative reputation for you, which can be incredibly challenging to get away from once it has been rooted in. You must always think about the good of all, especially if you will be using the analysis to get your way.

CHAPTER 9
Beware Of Cluster Gestures

Cluster gestures is a term used to describe rapid, deviated gestures that a person engages in. These are often quick, short-lived deviations from their baseline that indicate a certain mood or perception toward whichever topic the cluster gestures have happened around. The FBI uses cluster gestures as a way to identify someone's guilt, or other emotional cues, surrounding specific information. This way, they can often tell if someone is lying, covering something up, or feeling guilty about something being discussed with them by the interrogation officers.

Although cluster gestures are commonly looked for by the FBI, they are not exclusively seen in people that are feeling guilty or lying to cover something up. Cluster gestures can also be seen around positive topics and used in positive ways. The primary thing to know about cluster gestures is that the behavior itself is merely a deviation away from baseline for a quick moment. A person will either immediately return to baseline because they want to cover something up or because the overall experience is not about that one topic, so there is no need to retain the emotions or thoughts around it.

Cluster Gestures Occur Around Specific Topics

There are multiple occasions where you might be talking with someone, and the conversation drifts across many different topics. In fact, virtually every conversation you have is likely to drift around multiple topics, even if you are only enjoying short-lived conversations. For example, if you were ordering a coffee at a café, you might start with your order then move on to small talk about the weather or another simple topic. Baseline conversations always deviate, just like people's emotions do.

Cluster gestures can be used as a way to get to know someone better or as a way to get more information out of a person. If you are getting to know someone better, pay close attention to how their gestures are surrounding different topics or pieces of information. This will indicate how they feel about those topics and what their general perspective is toward them. If you are using cluster gestures as a way to get more information out of someone, you will purposefully bring up specific topics to discuss with them so you can monitor their gestures around that topic. This is how authorities use cluster gestures to determine if someone is lying or not, which enables them to prod deeper or dig into other psychological measures to draw information out of potential victims, witnesses, or perpetrators.

If you are using gestures to get to know someone better, you may want to lead the conversation through different topics so you can get to know them from multiple perspectives. You might talk a bit about everything from the wheel of life, which allows you to get a rounded view of who they are, or you may focus exclusively on the parts of the wheel that are relevant to your relationship with that person. The wheel of life defines the eight primary categories of our lives, and it includes health, wealth, career, relationships, love, relationship to yourself, hobbies, and faith.

Suppose you are using cluster gestures as a way to get to know information about a specific topic, such as if you want to know if someone likes something or if they are lying, you want to intentionally bring that topic up and pay close attention to their reaction. If their reaction is neutral, chances are you will not walk away with sufficient information to make your choice. If, however, their reaction is positive or negative, you will walk away with enough knowledge to get a general understanding of their stance on a given subject. This is particularly useful when it comes to surprising someone or catching someone in a lie.

The Type Of Gestures Reveals The Mystery

The way to read the cluster gestures is to pay close attention to the specific types of gestures they are using. You will read their body language, facial expressions, eyes, and emotional energy just as you would in any other circumstance; however, you want to be particularly attentive as cluster gestures are fleeting. If you are prompting them purposefully, you want to do so when you are ready to pay close attention, so you get an adequate analysis for the moment. In many cases, you will see cluster gestures unexpectedly, as this happens on a regular basis and is not always something you have to be looking for or encouraging. Of course, you can use these random moments to deepen your knowledge about someone, which will make your understanding of them more complete. Or, at the very least, it will teach you more about human behavior.

If you are looking to learn about topics that make someone happy or feel positive in some way, pay attention to fleeting cluster gestures that indicate a positive deviation from their baseline. Smiles, eyebrow raises, bright eyes, leaning forward, laughing, or seeming lost in a daydream for a few moments are all great ways to identify a positive reaction. Some people will outright admit to their thoughts or feelings, too, though it is helpful to pay close attention to *how* they admit them to ensure they are telling the truth. This is an excellent way to learn about what lights a person up or makes them feel good, which will allow you to use that information to your advantage. This may help you get your needs met, surprise them, or do something nice for them that helps them feel better if they are having a particularly bad time.

Suppose you are looking for negative deviations, such as if you want to catch someone in a lie, pay close attention to expressions that indicate fear, anxious surprise, anger, sadness, or contempt. A pinched brow, tight face, closed-off posture, or a person leaning away or becoming fidgety all indicates that a person is feeling negative toward a specific sentiment or topic. Sometimes, people may have these reactions because they are feeling guilty or lying about something. Other times, they may be simply expressing distaste or displeasure toward something you have been discussing. Consider the overall conversation and the context behind it to get a clearer understanding of why someone has had a negative deviation, as this will give you greater insight into the thoughts and feelings behind the reaction.

Deviation May Help Uncover The Truth

Deviations are excellent for helping uncover the truth, especially in someone who may be particularly closed off or unwilling to admit to something. When you want to learn the truth from someone, there are three things you can do to leverage cluster gestures as a way to gain insight. You will prod the topic, pay attention to gestures, and recognize their follow up behaviors.

Whenever you prod the topic you want to know more about, it is always best to start small and work your way up. Immediately jumping into the main conversation can be intimidating and may cause someone to be caught off guard, which could make their immediate reaction less accurate. Rather than reacting to the topic itself, they may react to you charging head-first into an intimate or intense conversation.

Instead, you want to work your way there by asking smaller questions that skirt around the conversation itself. Then, you can start working toward the bigger questions. Use the cluster gestures and overall responses you get from the initial questions to guide you through the bigger or more intense questions, never moving faster than the other person is willing to give up information both verbally and nonverbally.

Paying attention to gestures means you have to pay close attention to their body, face, and eyes. Eyes will be the fastest gestures to come and go, followed by the face, then the body. Most people can easily hold a non-assuming posture but struggle to control their face and struggle even more to control their eyes. For that reason, you should look from the eyes to the face, to the body, which ensures that you gain the most information possible. You can immediately begin to uncover what these gestures mean if your knowledge and intuition can guide you, or you can keep track of them in your mind and reflect on them later for deeper understanding. Often, both methods can be used to deepen your insight, if need be.

Lastly, you need to pay attention to their follow up. Someone that is trying to hide something or that has a negative feeling about something will often do their best to change the conversation to something more enjoyable, or they might try to end the conversation altogether.

Alternatively, someone that likes or enjoys something will attempt to have the conversation linger on that topic longer so they can derive more joy from it. A person's follow up will help reinforce their gestures, so pay attention and factor it into your insight when you determine what their actions genuinely mean.

CHAPTER 10
Compare And Contrast What You Discover

The more you observe people and their body language, the more you will discover the meaning of their body language and the best way to interpret it. Recognizing baselines is imperative, yet baselines are irrelevant if you are not using them as they are intended to be used. The purpose of a baseline is to formulate an initial observation about what someone's body language means and how this contributes to their identity profile. Following that initial observation, you need to discover how and why that individual deviates away from their baseline so you can understand their unique body language tendencies.

Believe it or not, body language does have variations from person to person. Similarly to how people speak with varying types of slang, body language can have differences, too. Each person will have their own unique expressions that indicate when they are pleased, annoyed, interested, enraged, and so forth. Recognizing each individual's unique expressions is an excellent way to identify what their body language means and read it more accurately.

The Difference Between Personality And Deviation

Observing the difference between personality and true body language deviations is important because not everyone communicates in the same ways. If you assume everyone communicates the same, you will misinterpret many signals based on irrelevant or inaccurate baseline findings. Instead, you must identify the differences between personality and deviation.

Personality describes the specific ways someone communicates or the body language signals they are most likely to use to communicate with you. For example, a person with a confident personality is likely to use many hand gestures and strong poses, while a person that lacks confidence is likely to stay close to themselves and small in their movements. Knowing this prevents you from misinterpreting a confident person's body language as aggressive or a person without confidence's body language as disinterested because you are aware that the nature of their movements is based on personality, not their mood.

True deviations express an actual shift in emotion or mood that a person experiences. For example, if a person that is typically confident suddenly starts showing signals that they lack confidence, you know they have deviated. These deviations give you significant insight into how a person thinks or feels by showing you that it moves them enough to cause them to actually deviate away from their "normal." These deviations are where you gain the ability to identify the best ways to interact with people. For example, if you want to stimulate a certain emotional response, you can use known triggers to do so. Or, if you want to stimulate more of the same, you can use the necessary triggers.

Each time you meet a new person or start talking to someone, first look for their baseline and personality, then look for deviations. This way, you can clearly interpret each signal and understand what it means, as well as how it will affect your communication with that individual.

Discovering Body Language Nuances

There are two excellent strategies you can use to help you identify body language nuances between different people. Identifying this is essential to discovering people's true baseline, as it allows you to recognize their exact baseline in relation to them. The first strategy allows you to identify nuances and personality differences in an individual, while the second strategy allows you to identify these things over groups of people.

Identifying an individual's nuances is an excellent way to personalize your methods of approaching them and interacting with them based on their personality. When you have a deeper awareness of how someone is and what their methods of expression are, it becomes easier to interpret each of their expressions without questions lingering in your mind as to whether you interpreted correctly or not. You can identify these expressions by observing the person over time, especially in relation to how they react or respond to different triggers in their life. Consider paying close attention to triggers that would typically stimulate an emotional reaction out of someone, and identify how they react to that trigger. Common triggers include stressful situations, hunger, funny jokes, a peaceful view, relaxation, and more. The more you understand a person's natural reactions to different emotions, the easier it will be for you to interpret their thoughts and feelings and the scale to which they are experiencing them.

Identifying an individual's expressions is helpful in that it allows you to understand that person in a more significant manner. However, it is not reasonable to expect yourself to be able to fully understand an individual's nuances and standard body language and behavioral expressions. For example, if you are on a first date with someone, or if you are in a sales meeting, you do not have limitless time to identify how that person communicates and also make an in-depth profile of them. You must learn to read and identify nuances quickly if you want to use body language to your advantage in a more accurate manner. This is where profiling comes in.

Profiling is a practice where you observe as many people as possible, and, as you do, you categorize them. You will rapidly see that people with similar personalities tend to have similar body expressions, too, which means they can be profiled together. Profiling does not guarantee that you have an exact understanding of each individual you meet, but it does provide you with a more complex and accurate baseline of which to interpret people. It also allows you to better understand their deviations, as you are aware of which deviations are likely and normal and how exactly to interpret them based on that person's personality.

Analyzing Each Person's Natural Expressions

Analyzing each person's natural expressions requires patience, as you must be willing to give yourself time to witness these different expressions. One way to do this, especially if you have a significant amount of time with each individual, is to observe their natural reactions to life. This is where you will get the most accurate, in-depth understanding of people's body language because you are observing them in their natural habitat, responding to natural triggers. However, you might not have all the time in the world to observe someone in their natural habitat and wait for each emotion to be naturally invoked.

Once again, dating and sales are two great examples of this. When dating someone, you need to be able to generally identify who they are and how they behave rapidly to determine whether it is worth it for you to go on further dates. In sales, you need to be able to profile someone, so you know how to sell your product or service to them effectively rapidly. Knowing how to prompt people to react to different emotional triggers in a natural way exposes you to their different emotional reactions and gives you the opportunity to understand how their reactions are. The key is you must be in control so you are getting these emotional reactions at the right time, rather than accidentally activating them in a way that has that person thinking they should not be talking to or trusting you any longer.

To prompt someone to express body language relating to a certain emotion, say something that you believe is likely to pull a specific emotional trigger. It is best if you do this based on something they already said to ensure that your desired emotion is triggered. Using something they mentioned upsets them, inspires them, makes them happy, or stimulates any other emotion in them, and says a few things about it. Better yet, ask a question, so they have to engage and think about it. If you do this correctly, they will think in such a way that triggers a specific emotional reaction, and that reaction will help you identify their body language surrounding different emotions.

It is essential to note that the body language they use indicates a lot about how they feel about themselves, too. For example, let's say you elicit feelings of frustration in someone. If you are speaking with a confident person, they will likely expand their body language by puffing out their chest or making themselves appear bigger, which is done as a way to assert their authority and their willingness to protect themselves.

Alternatively, if you are speaking with someone that lacks confidence, they may try to shrink their body language, or they might appear anxious because they do not like to deal with confrontation and anger. Noting the differences is an excellent way to create profiles in your mind so you can adequately interpret different people's body language and signals.

Observing Deviations In Relation To Triggers

To observe someone's deviations in relation to triggers, you must first anticipate what their likely triggers are. Everyone has their own triggers, but most people will have similarities in what triggers them. Family, money, and love or marriage are common triggers in people's lives. Triggers can also be far more specific, such as someone's inability to use a new piece of technology, their favorite food, or an experience they had recently that made them feel either positive or negative.

Anticipating people's likely triggers means you can identify times when they are most likely to deviate from their baseline. You know the minute those triggers are pulled, an emotional response is about to occur, which means you will be able to observe the deviation in their body, face, and movements. You might also pull these triggers on purpose by naturally burying them in your conversation to see what types of emotional responses are gained.

When you observe for deviations, you must pay close attention as deviations can be fleeting, especially if someone is using cluster gestures as a way to cover something up. If you miss someone's cues or signals, you may need to wait for another opportunity to observe them so you understand them better.

If you are purposefully stimulating someone's triggers to create emotional responses, be sure to do so intentionally. For example, in sales, if you are trying to trigger need by stimulating frustration and then offering a solution, pay close attention. You do not want to stimulate too many different emotions, nor do you want to create excess frustration because this makes it seem as though you are intentionally trying to manipulate them. In that case, no one will trust you, and through that, you will lose your capacity to stimulate any emotions other than skepticism and disinterest or frustration toward you.

CHAPTER 11
Observe Mirrored Behaviors

Mirrored behaviors are a unique, interesting form of body language that provides significant insight into how a person thinks or feels about you, specifically. This allows you to move away from reading exclusively about how someone feels about different topics or interests and instead allows you the opportunity to get a better understanding of where you stand with that person. Although this may make it seem deep, mirrored behaviors are not something that requires you to know someone extensively for it to happen. Total strangers may mirror your behavior, as will people you are intentionally engaging with and people you have known for a long time.

When you experience mirrored behaviors, it means the other person is particularly interested in you. The way they mirror your behaviors, the amount they do so, and the specific behaviors they choose to mimic all help you interpret what they actually mean. It helps to understand the context of the situation, the person, and the way they are mirroring you, as this allows you to truly understand where you stand with that person. Mirrored behavior means someone has seen you, taken an interest in you, and is now mirroring your body language. This subconscious behavior makes it obvious that the other person is interested in you and engaged at the moment because they are quite literally mimicking you. Mirrored behavior can happen in physical body language, as well as tonality and speech patterns. The person exhibiting mirrored behavior is engaged with the other person, while the person leading the behavior is generally the one with the upper hand in that conversation. Unless, of course, both parties are mirroring each other's behavior, which shows mutual attraction and interest.

You can observe mirrored behavior in others, as well as yourself. Observing this behavior in yourself may seem strange, as you are becoming self-aware of your own subconscious cues, and it might even feel funny as you realize you are essentially copying the person you are communicating with. Of course, this is a good sign you are on the same page as this person, and it keeps you engaged and subconsciously flatters them, so long as you are not obvious or exaggerated about it. There are four significant times which you might observe mirrored behavior: on a date, during a sale, in general, in everyday life, or in yourself.

Dating And Mirrored Behavior

Looking for mirrored behaviors on a date is an excellent way to gauge how well the date is going and whether it's worth it for you to plan future dates with this person. Romantically speaking, you want a person to be engaged with you and showing interest if you will date them again;

otherwise, you risk investing in someone that is not equally invested in you, which can be a painful experience.

When you go on a date with someone, and they mirror your behavior, it is a sure sign that they are interested in you and are enjoying themselves. Your date is unlikely to be aware of their behavior, so do not go out of your way to point it out to them. Doing so may make them feel uncomfortable and can break the mood and make you both feel awkward. Instead, simply observe it and use it as a sign that they are interested in you or, at the very least, attracted to you.

Observing mirrored behavior in your date's body language will be much easier than observing it elsewhere. They might smile when you smile, touch their hair when you touch yours, or move their arm the same way you do, all without even realizing they are doing it. These are all easy for you to pick up on as you pay attention to their body and what they are doing with it. In verbal language, however, observing mirroring behaviors takes more practice. Mirrored behavior often involves the other person using similar words as you, as well as a similar tone of voice. For example, if you often say "No way!" excitedly, and you say something to your date, and they say "No way!" with excitement in their tone, you can feel confident that a person is attracted to you and interested in knowing more about you.

Mirrored Behavior And Sales

Salespeople often use mirrored behavior as a way to gauge the level of interest of their audience, as well as to identify the exact moment that one should pitch their sale. When a client is mirroring your body language, it means they are interested in what you have to say and are eager to learn more. The sooner a person starts mirroring your body language, and the more engaged they are, the easier they will be to sell to. This doesn't mean you should get complacent or assume they are an automatic yes; however, it does signify that this client has significant potential to become a purchasing client.

Using mirrored behavior in sales means identifying how you can use it to pinpoint the exact moment you should make your pitch. This means you must observe not only mirrored behavior but also the amount of mirrored behavior being expressed. You must observe carefully to pinpoint the moment mirrored behavior starts and to track it so you can identify when it becomes more frequent. Once a person is frequently mirroring your behavior and matching your expressions, you know they are ready for you to pitch to.

With sales, mirrored behavior is less likely to be sensual in nature. Unlike with dates, where your date may focus on their hair or grooming themselves, your client is more likely to mimic your excited and happy behaviors. They might smile, mimic your hand gestures, or match your words as a way to show they are engaged in your pitch. All of this will be happening subconsciously, so they are unlikely to realize they have changed their expressions at all. Of course, don't point this out. Instead, quietly observe and use it to help you pace the conversation and pitch your offer.

Mirrored Behavior In General

Outside of dating and sales, mirrored behavior can still happen. Often, it signifies attraction or interest in someone, so you are most likely to notice it when you engage with someone who is invested in you at that moment. The most common place to see mirrored behavior in your everyday life is amongst your friends and family, though you may also see it between coworkers, especially if you are in competition with any of them. With friends or family, mirrored behaviors are an expression of the mutual love shared between you and the people you care about and can be seen as endearing and an affirmation of your connection.

With coworkers that you are in competition with, not ones you are friends with, mirrored behaviors indicate they want to be like you, but better. Essentially, they are mirroring the behaviors they see you engaging in that boost your likelihood of succeeding, then adding their own added abilities to make themselves look better. In this case, mirrored behavior is conscious, not subconscious, because that person is intentionally trying to mimic your behaviors.

One other time you might see mimicry or mirrored behaviors is with someone that looks up to you. When people look up to you or idolize you, they start mimicking your behaviors because they desire to be just like you. This is a wonderful example of "mimicry is the highest form of flattery" because it implies that they are inspired by you and want to be more like you.

Mirroring Other's Behavior

Mirroring another person's behavior on purpose is an excellent way to gain someone's attention or get them more invested in you. Just as someone's subconscious mind is responsible for them mirroring you, their subconscious mind also interprets your mirrored behaviors of them and uses it to reinforce that they are liked at that moment. They can see you are invested in them, and they become more invested in you as a result. This is an excellent way to gain someone's investment by mildly mirroring their behavior until they start to do it back, which means they are paying attention and interested.

If you choose to use mirrored behaviors to support your ability to attract engagement from others, you must be careful. Excessive mirroring or using strange behaviors in an effort to motivate mirroring are both unnatural ways that people attempt to identify this type of behavior, and that can sabotage your communications. You must learn to infuse this practice into natural communication to avoid confusing people or driving them away.

It is important to mirror behaviors relevant to the context of your meeting, too, to avoid using behaviors that are unnatural to the circumstances. For example, if you are on a date, mirror your date when they smile, groom their hair, or fix their clothes. Or, if you are in a sales meeting, mirror your client any time they use certain hand gestures, words, or facial expressions. This way, you match in a way that is appropriate to the circumstances, which makes them feel even more invested in a positive way. Once someone is mirroring you consistently, you do not have to worry about mirroring them back, as you have now gained their investment.

CHAPTER 12
Identify The Strong Voice

Each person has their own unique voice, or the voice they use on a regular basis. Discovering their strong voice, or primary voice, allows you to learn more about this person based on what you hear in the sound of their voice. Each person expresses a great deal about themselves, from their personality to their self-perception and emotions, which is why their voices are so valuable. Knowing what someone's voice means, means you can use it to help you interpret that person and gain insight into them through your conversation.

Like with body language, voices have a baseline (strong voice) and deviations. Knowing the baseline of someone's voice means you can identify their deviations. How you interpret these deviations are just like interpreting deviations in physical gestures: as long as you know what is normal, you can identify what isn't and listen for cues to understand *why* it was no longer normal. Most often, emotions or beliefs are the driving force behind deviations and provide ample reason for someone to suddenly start speaking or sounding different.

The Meaning Of Tonality And Why It Matters

Tonality refers to a person's voice, and the tone of their voice reflects their different emotions and characteristics. You can identify a person's tonality through written language, as well as the spoken language. A person's baseline tonality gives you the opportunity to better understand their average personality, while their deviations allow you to interpret their emotions and perceptions around different topics, just like with body language.

It is important to understand that tonality changes a lot under different circumstances. For example, the way your voice sounds when you talk to your family will be far different from how it sounds when you talk to your boss. These different tones are used to assert different emotions while also positioning yourself in different roles. With your family, you might be positioning yourself casually, while with your boss, you might be positioning yourself as a confident worker.

Just as your tonality will change, so will others tones. Listening for variances allows you to identify how a person likely sees themselves in relation to another person, how they want to come across to that person, and what emotion they are feeling at that moment. This is important, as the more you understand a person, the easier it is to relate to them and use this relation to gain what you want from them.

Interpreting someone's tonality is essential to the process of analyzing people because of the amount of knowledge you gain from this form of analysis. While body language and facial expressions may prove tough to interpret from time to time, tonality is almost always easy to identify and read. Your brain subconsciously knows how to interpret most tones, and you can use certain expressions and indicators to ensure that you have interpreted it correctly.

Another reason why interpreting tonality is so important is that, in our modern world, distant communications are common. We tend to spend more time talking on the phone, texting, or connecting over social media or email than we do talking to people in person. Knowing how to interpret tonality through text and written language means you can better understand that person from a distance and use that to your advantage for whatever you might need it for.

Identifying A Person's Typical Tone

Identifying a person's typical tone is as important as identifying their baseline body language, as it provides you the opportunity to understand what their "normal" is. Knowing their normal immediately indicates what personality archetype they have and what you can likely expect out of that person. This way, you can anticipate reactions to different emotional triggers and use their baseline to determine whether their reaction was normal to their behavior or not. You can also use this to identify the occurrence of a reaction in the first place, which can be especially helpful when you want or need to stimulate specific reactions out of people. Even when you don't, witnessing this allows you to understand that person with greater context and dynamics.

The easiest way to identify a person's typical tone is to strike up a conversation with them and listen. Talk about everything from small talk topics to topics that are more relevant to the context of your meeting, and listen to see how they come across. What personality traits can you identify through their tone? How do you think they position themselves in the conversation, based on how they sound? Is there anything to indicate that they are feeling affected by something beyond the conversation and that they may be bringing that forth with them? You can interpret all of these answers based on the projection of their voice, the emotions you pick up on, and how readily willing they are to speak to you.

If you are speaking online or through text, pay attention to how their punctuation looks, which words they are using, and what they have said overall. Emojis are another great way to interpret tone, as people who use a lot of emojis tend to have more whimsical or light-hearted personalities and will directly convey their intended emotion or tone through the emojis they add to their conversation. However, emojis are not always appropriate to the communication forum, so be aware of people using them inappropriately as this may indicate they are not taking something seriously or are uneducated in that style of communication.

The Common Triggers Of Tonality

Once you know someone's baseline, you can identify anytime their tonality changes from what you have come to see as being normal. Change in tonality gives you two things: the opportunity to know more about a person and the opportunity to gauge them. When it comes to getting to know a person, change in tonality gives you more context behind their methods of interacting and allows you to identify how they feel and view themselves in different circumstances. This is a great way to have more compassion, a deeper understanding, or a more significant ability to anticipate a person. When it comes to gauging them, tonality allows you to identify how a person feels at that moment to see whether it is worth it for you to make a pitch. So, if you are selling something or want to receive something from someone, you can use their tone to determine whether they're ready or not.

There are many things that will trigger tonality change. The four most likely triggers are other people, circumstances, their location, or the context in which they have shown up for something.

Other people trigger a change in tonality because the person who is talking views themselves differently around others, so their role changes. For example, at one moment, they may be playing the role of parent, while in another, they may be the friend or the confidante. As their role changes, their tone changes, too, to match the role they have taken on.

Circumstances trigger a change in tonality by first triggering the emotions a person experiences. Specific circumstances might also cause a person to pick a new role in relation to the circumstance, which further stimulates change. For example, in a casual setting, someone might sound casual, but as soon as they are presented with a task to complete, they take on a more authoritative role.

Location triggers change in tonality based on habit. People usually associate different locations with different roles in their lives, which they tend to click into regardless of whether they are actively in need of playing out that role or not. For example, at home, you might continue to be authoritative and parental, even if your children are not around because you habitually associate home with parenting.

Context triggers change in tonality by giving the person a story, or a reason, behind why they have shown up for something. When a person has a story in mind about why they have shown up, they formulate a role to suit that story, and they partake in that role. For example, if you call a friend over for a casual dinner, they will likely show up in a casual manner, but if you call them over to vent about something difficult you have faced, they might show up with a more concerned or focused tone.

Discovering The Meaning Of Their Tone

Observing the meaning of someone's tonality gives you the opportunity to use that tone to formulate an assumption about that person. This does not guarantee your assumption is right, but it allows you to use that assumption as a baseline so you can then look for clues to determine if you were right or not. You discover the meaning of someone's tone by observing their tone and listening for specific cues about what their tone actually is in any given moment.

There are five essential types of tones when it comes to communication, all of which give you ample insight into how a person is feeling or perceiving themselves in any circumstance. The five tones include motivator, educator, coach, colleague, and caretaker. People may often match two or more of these descriptions at any moment; however, they will always have one primary tone in each setting. Which primary tone will change based on their triggers, too, so observe for these changes to gain more information about someone.

The tone of the motivator often sounds like an inspirational person. They tend to say things that are uplifting and inspiring, and their voice comes across as cheery and hopeful. You can hear the cheer in their voice based on the sheer energy behind it, and they tend to project their voice with certainty and excitement. A motivator sounds enthused about everything. Depending on who they are talking to, they may be motivational in that they are coaching someone else to achieve greatness, or motivational in that they are motivated to receive coaching from someone else to achieve greatness. A great example of a motivator would be Michelle Obama or Oprah Winfrey, both of which are excellent at inspiring others through their tonality and expressions.

Educator tonality indicates that someone knows something and wants to inform others. Their voice is full of authority, and they speak in affirmatives. They make statements more than anything else, and when they ask a question, it is intentional and to reinforce their point. An educator will rarely speak with elation or excitement because these two might indicate they are not in control or in a position of authority. Instead, they have a rather consistent tone, and the ends of their sentences tend to have a consistent pitch, rather than an upturn in the pitch of their voice. A great example of an educator would be Martin Luther King Jr., who was a motivational educator. His primary communication style was as an educator, as he informed people of what was going on and used this information to inspire change.

A coaching tone sounds directive and assertive and will vary depending on whether it is uplifting or demanding based on the coach's personality. Because it is directive and assertive, it often sounds like a coach is bossing you around or making commands, rather than pausing to receive feedback. A positive coach recognizes that their role is to lead everyone else, so they will confidently tell everyone what to do. If they are an excellent coach, they will ask for feedback and receive input from their team to ensure they are directing them in a way that motivates their team to listen and take action. The inclusion of this spoken behavior indicates they are a caring coach that sees themselves as a part of the team rather than an authoritative coach that sees themselves as being above the team. An excellent example of a coach is Tony Robbins, who knows how to communicate to get everyone involved while also operating as a part of his team, rather than being above his team.

The tonality of a colleague is one that is chatty and informal, and that sees you as being equal to them. They often speak similarly to you and will have a neutral or uplifted tone in their voice as they come across as friendly and warm. You know a colleague feels equal to you because they will inspire you while also being inspired by you. Virtually everything about your communication is equal, which means they view you as being on the same level as they are. Because of this, your communication is balanced and often rather enjoyable while also being potentially insightful and helpful. An excellent example of a colleague is your best friend or your closest workmate, both of which will likely speak to you in a casual, informal manner.

If someone has a caretaker tone, their tone comes across as concerned and careful. Their voice almost sounds whiny as they ask if you are ok and try to help you through whatever trouble you may be facing. They sound concerned, often speak in a higher pitch, and will say things that indicate they are willing to take care of you mentally, emotionally, or physically. A caretaker sees themselves as being responsible for others and feels the need to look after everyone around them. If a caretaker takes this tone on in appropriate circumstances, such as when they are parenting, they see themselves as being responsible for another and are genuinely caring. If they take this role on when it is seemingly inappropriate, such as with their boss or a colleague, it indicates that they see themselves as less than and believe they are responsible for everyone. This is a good sign that they feel unworthy or uncomfortable around others. A great example of a caretaker would be one of your parents, which allows you to observe the nuances in their caretaking behaviors and tones throughout the process of caring for you in different circumstances.

CHAPTER 13
Pay Attention To Their Walk

You can tell a significant amount about a person based on the way they walk. Everything from the way they stand to the way they move their body while walking reveal key factors about their personality and who they likely are. Each of us has our own walk and will put our own flair and style into it. The way that flair or style comes across is how you determine what a person's walk genuinely says about them.

As with anything else, the way a person walks can change based on the context of the situation and the way they are feeling. For example, a generally peppy person that is feeling sad or disempowered may suddenly start to walk more slouched over and slow, or a generally shy person that is feeling confident or empowered may start to walk taller and with greater authority. Paying attention to someone's normal and deviations from normal, then, is still a key role in reading someone's walk properly.

Aside from paying attention to baselines and deviations, there are seven key pieces of information you can gain from a person's walk. These pieces of information give you an insight into their personality, behaviors, and tendencies and can help you make more sense of a person in your life. You can also use these factors to help you create a walk that communicates precisely what you want people to think about you, allowing you to have a subconscious impact on the way people perceive you.

Their Speed Correlates To Their Energy

The speed at which someone walks says a great deal about the amount of energy they bring to their lives or at least the amount of energy they are bringing at that moment. If a person typically walks faster, this indicates that they generally have high energy and are highly outgoing. Fast walkers have actually been studied and reported as being more conscientious, having a lower rate of neuroticism, and higher rates of extraversion. They also tend to be more open to the world around them and are excellent socializers. If you are looking for an outgoing, life-of-the-party type person, look for someone that moves fast. If someone suddenly starts moving faster, though they generally walk slower, this may indicate one of two things. They may suddenly have improved energy and are feeling good about something, or they may be anxious or worried about something.

It is important to note the type of fastness that we're looking for here. Fast yet graceful indicates that said individual typically walks faster; therefore, they are naturally more outgoing. If a person is walking fast and lacks grace, however, either because they are stumbling or they just plain look strange doing it, this indicates they do not generally walk fast. Chances are, this is someone that is trying to get somewhere in a hurry.

Slow Speed Indicates A Cautious Personality

A person that walks at a particularly slow pace or that tends to stroll when they walk, no matter where they are walking, is someone that tends to have a more cautious personality. This person feels uncertain and uncomfortable about things; therefore, they are walking slower, so they have more time to process and create feelings of safety. People that walk slowly as a sign of cautiousness are generally not expressing that they are suddenly troubled; rather, they are genuinely slower, more cautious people that require more time to figure things out. If a person suddenly starts walking slower than normal, this might indicate they are upset or feeling down about something.

In addition to a slower overall pace, a person that is generally more cautious will take shorter steps. It is as though they are truly trying to move forward slowly, the way one might carefully step toward the edge of a high cliff or across a balance beam when they are feeling unsteady. They want time to pace themselves and come to terms with each step, rather than to rush through it. This type of person is generally measured, fiercely independent, and self-centered, though this may not mean they experience these tendencies in a negative way. For example, they may be self-centered but not self-serving, meaning they do tend to focus on themselves, but they are still kind and caring toward others.

If They're Anxious, They Veer To The Left

A person that is feeling anxious may be obvious in their hunched shoulders, reduced space expenditure, and fidgety behavior. Even if they manage to calm themselves enough that they're not taking fast, short strides, a person that is feeling anxious can still be identified by their walk. Their key identifying factor is that, if they are anxious, they will veer to the left. This is true whether they are generally anxious overall or just anxious in that particular moment.

This peculiar insight was gained when researchers placed a blindfold over people's eyes and had them walk around in an empty room. Those that were feeling anxious tended to veer to the left while no one else did. Researchers proposed this may be the case because, during a moment of anxiety, the right side of your brain works harder than the left side of your brain as it has to manage the instance of doubt and dread. Regardless of whether that's true or not, you can observe this in people in real life, too.

Confidence Can Be Seen In A Saunter

Sauntering can be seen by anyone that walks slow and easy, with a sense of swagger in their step. They walk as though they are the coolest person in the world because, in their worlds, they are the coolest. These individuals have a high sense of self-confidence and believe greatly in themselves and their abilities. You might assume this to be reserved for high-end professionals and athletes, yet this can actually be seen in any type of human.

The walk of confidence cannot be missed because of how tall and significant it is. In fact, we are so accustomed to seeing and interpreting this walk as confidence that many therapists have begun using this as a way to improve their client's confidence. They start by having the client visualize themselves walking with confidence, then move toward having them walk this way in real life. As the client grows used to seeing themselves this way with visualization, they feel a greater sense of self-confidence. As they grow used to walking this way, they experience biofeedback that tells their brain that they are confident; therefore, they feel a more significant sense of confidence.

Agitated Walkers Are Detail-Oriented

People that walk with a sense of agitation, or like they are harried, have quick bursts of energy in their walk. They tend to move fast, to the point where they almost look fidgety or reactive. Often, they are doing more than just walking, too. They may be fixing their clothes, checking their bag, texting, talking on the phone, reaching for a taxi, or doing all of these things at once. People that walk this way are reported as having greater attention to detail than the average person, which is why their brains are always running so fast.

In addition to walking with a seeming sense of agitation or excess energy, these walkers tend to jump into action faster than anyone else, too. They are the first to jump up and open the door, pull out a chair for someone, or shake someone's hand. Their quick, jerky walking style pivots their attention from one place to another as they go, and that helps their thoughts race through their mind, too. These people are highly effective and productive, which makes them excellent professionals or people to have in charge of special projects.

Self-Esteem Can Be Witnessed In Grace

The amount of self-esteem a person experiences can be directly witnessed in a person's grace. Still, this is not always the most accurate way to tell someone's self-confidence levels, as many people are excellent at mimicking grace as a way to appear more confident than they actually are. It is said, however, that a person that walks more gracefully tends to have a greater sense of self-esteem and self-confidence.

Beyond gracefully gliding through each step, you will actually witness this type of person display grace in their posture, too. Their toes will be intentionally pointed, they seem to swiftly carry their whole body through with each step, and they look as though they are dancing as they walk. This type of walking is said to be unnatural to our bodies, which means a person must learn to intentionally walk this way, thus affirming their high self-esteem and self-confidence.

The Position Of Their Shoulders Says This...

Lastly, the position of someone's shoulders says a lot about how they are feeling. A person that walks with tall, squared shoulders likely feels confident in themselves, at least to the point of intentionally correcting their posture as they walk. A person that walks with tall, casual shoulders naturally feels good about themselves, as this is how they genuinely walk and are not postured intentionally. A person that walks with their shoulders down or slumped is trying to protect themselves. The position of their shoulders indicates they are trying to physically protect their hearts because they are vulnerable or they carry hurt around them.

Sometimes, people that have recently experienced trauma or something that reduces their self-esteem or mood will begin walking with slumped shoulders. Often, this is a temporary change and will revert back once they heal, though this may become their new normal if the experience was traumatizing enough.

CHAPTER 14
Be Aware Of Action Words

The words people choose when communicating with others' say a lot about their personality. Unlike other forms of body language or communication, the specific words people use to communicate and describe things typically remain the same. For this reason, it is helpful to be mindful of action words, as well as any words a person frequently uses, as this all indicates how they think and who they are.

Action words become particularly helpful when you have someone describe something. For example, if you are out with a friend and ask them to describe how their day went, the specific words they use will say a lot about what they genuinely think about their answer. Using their word choice to analyze them and what they mean is an excellent way to gain context into how they actually think or feel about something. Thus, you gain the opportunity to either know them more or use their own language to communicate with them more effectively.

What "I" Really Means About You

The word "I" says more about people than they tend to realize. In fact, the impact it has on our perception of ourselves and other people's perception of us is massive. Yet, many people do not realize this because of the impact it is having, and the experience of saying "I" itself are two highly subconscious experiences. You do not realize how often you say it, and others tend not to realize how frequently they hear it; instead, they just pick up on a "vibe" from you.

The vibe they're picking up on is often quite selfish. Saying "I" frequently indicates that you are focused more on yourself than anything, which means you may be expressing the fact that you are subordinate to everyone around you. By saying "I" frequently, others can tell that you are fixated on yourself, which generally means you are feeling anxious, self-conscious, or insecure. In fixating on yourself, you hope to shield yourself by owning your flaws and explaining them away to the best of your ability, which allows you to feel as though you are protected. Despite this fact, you might otherwise come across as confident. This is because people that are insecure are often trying the hardest to appear as though they are not, which is why they come across as arrogant and egotistical since their confidence is not rooted and genuine.

People that avoid the word "I" are found as being higher powered and as having significant confidence. They have so much confidence in themselves that they do not need to think about themselves or worry excessively about their self-awareness. Rather than busying themselves with the worry of how they are and what they look like, they are excited about the world outside of themselves and are looking for ways to engage in it. They tend to say "you" and "we" more or will use sentences that do not refer to anyone in particular, whatsoever.

Slang And Casual Language

Slang and casual language play a significant role in the way people view us. Our slang and casual language are influenced by our location, culture, or religion, the people we hang out with most, and our interests. On a grander scale, slang says more about our origin story than anything else. When we get down to specific types of slang, though, or "niche" slang, then we start revealing aspects of our personality traits or interests.

The degree to which our slang creates our origin story depends on how similarly we talk to the people in our locale. For example, people from New York talk far differently from people in Los Angeles. Likewise, people in the United States talk differently from people in Canada or Europe. These wider-scale nuances indicate where we are from, and to a trained ear, may even indicate where we are from in our locale. An excellent example would be the many vernaculars from New York, as people from different neighborhoods speak quite differently. If you were not from New York, you might recognize differences but not know what they mean. If you were a regular in New York, though, you would be able to tell which neighborhood they were from solely based on the way a person spoke.

Niche slang can further your ability to profile people by giving you the opportunity to identify their interests and the type of people they hang out with. For example, someone that hangs out with people in the music industry and that loves producing audio would use slang words that were associated with music, audio, and pop culture. Their use of these words would far exceed anyone that was not genuinely interested in this industry.

Listening to the slang words a person uses, as well as their casual language, allows you to understand more about who they are and where they come from. Once you put together their origin with their likely interests, you get a clearer understanding of what their personality is like, what they are interested in, and what they value or cherish. All of this can be used to gain context around a person's personality and show you the ways to connect with that person effectively.

Action Words That Declare Values

Action words declare things in someone's life or give you some insight into what they value. In conversations, action words describe things. People tend to use specific describing words or action words that hint toward their personality while also giving you the opportunity to understand more of what they value in life.

To identify someone's personality through action words, pay close attention to the types of words they use to describe the things that happen in their life. They may describe very few things, suggesting they are closed, cautious, and disinterested in what they are talking about. Or, they may describe many things while using colorful language to describe said things, which indicates they are fascinated, open, and engaged with the world around them. This may also indicate that they are a people pleaser or that they use highly open language to prevent people from asking more personal questions. This way, people think they know enough and do not need to ask anything more personal.

The average person will describe things, but not with extensive detail, and only when a description seems to naturally fit the conversation. The types of describing words they use indicate their generation, as well as the level of energy they bring with them in life. You may also discover what their personality is like, whether it is fun, flamboyant, proper, artistic, or otherwise, based on the types of action words they use.

To discover more of what they value in life, pay attention to where and when they use action words. The average person will only describe the things they care about and will provide more detail based on the amount they care about said thing. Listen to the types of words they use to describe said things to understand their energy around it, too. For example, if they use strong words filled with strong emotion, they are describing something they are seriously passionate about. If they describe things mildly and with casual emotion, this indicates they are interested in something, but not as extensively as they could be.

Matching People's Words

Matching people's words is a surprisingly common behavior, which falls under the category of mirrored behaviors. Couples can often tell which friend their spouse has been hanging out with recently, based on the language their partner is using when they return. When we like someone and have a good time with them, we tend to pick up the words they use and often incorporate them into our own language, too. We subconsciously talk the same way others' do as a way to create familiarity and a connection, and we often carry that into our own lives even once we are no longer around that other person. Often, we go back to our normal way of speaking after a few hours or days, though we may incorporate someone else's language into our own if we are particularly affectionate toward that person.

If you want to connect with someone intentionally, matching their words is an excellent way to do so. By describing things to them in a way they understand, and in the same way they would have described it, you connect with them. Through this, you know they understand you because you have said it in "their language." This way, they connect with you more, pay closer attention to what you are talking about, and have positive responses.

CHAPTER 15
Be Aware Of Personality Clues

Depending on what theory you look into, there are thousands of personality archetypes. However, the most popular theory in the world of psychology is the Jungian theory, which defines 12 Jungian archetypes. These 12 archetypes describe different personalities people are most likely to have, which allows you to have a better awareness of the type of people you are dealing with. Each personality type can be identified by key clues that indicate how that person is and who they are at their core. Of course, each archetype will have several subtypes that define the people within it; however, you will see massive similarities between these groups of people.

It is crucial to note that each person will likely fit into multiple personality type categories; however, they will have one that stands out above the rest. This personality type is the one you need to be aware of, as it indicates their overarching approach to life. If they have a strong secondary and tertiary personality type, use these to gain greater context around who they are and how they are.

The Ruler

The ruler is said to be a more independent type of person, and they thrive on having the most power possible. They want to be the leader, in control of everything around them. Their driving force is wanting control, and their goals involve prosperity and success in virtually every area of their lives. The ruler archetype uses their power as a strategy, and their greatest fear is chaos or being overthrown by the people they are leading. At their worst, the ruler can become highly authoritative to the point of it being destructive, and they struggle to delegate tasks. They are excellent with leadership and responsibility and work excellently in places of leadership. CEOs, bosses, aristocrats, politicians, role models, administrators, managers, and the monarchy are all known for having the ruler archetype.

The Artist

The artist is deeply in tune with their soul energy. They are excellent at imagining things and then promptly creating them. Often, they are seen as being the best at realizing visions or manifesting people's dreams into reality. Their fear would be mediocrity or execution, especially if it was caused by their creations. They use their artistic skill and control to manipulate the world around them, and they long to create cultures and express their vision to the world. The artist archetype tends to fall victim to their own perfectionism and may use bad solutions as a way to fix problems in their lives solely because those solutions provided space for creativity. When they are in their prime, artists are excellent with creativity and imagination and often find themselves in careers involving art, creation, invention, or planning.

The Sage

The sage is another self-driven person that tends to find themselves in isolation or independence more often than not. They are inspired by the truth and seek the truth in everything they do. Their intelligence and ability to analyze allow them to understand the world around them, and they use this as a strategy by seeking out information, engaging in self-reflection, and lusting after personal development and growth. They are terribly afraid of being duped, misled, or of falling victim to ignorance, especially if they themselves are the ignorant ones. Their weakness is that they can become trapped in analysis paralysis, but if they let that go, they are exceptional with offering wisdom and sharing their intelligence. The sage archetype commonly works in roles like scholars, teachers, detectives, advisors, planners, researchers, and anything to do with academics.

The Innocent

The innocent archetype is driven heavily by their ego. They want to be free to be themselves and desire freedom for everyone else, too. This archetype wants to get to paradise; they love living innocent and simplistic lifestyles, experiencing all of the good things the world has to offer. The number one goal of the innocent is to be happy, and they are afraid of being pushed to do something bad or wrong by the people in their lives. The strategy, often followed by an innocent person, is to do things right the first time because they do not want things to be done wrong. Because of how innocent they tend to be, this archetype is often seen as boring by others and rarely engages in things that others would deem fun or enjoyable. They are not the "life of the party" type. This archetype is particularly talented with faith and optimism and tends to be employed in traditional jobs such as teachers, lawyers, doctors, and so forth.

The Explorer

The explorer is a soul-driven person that loves to enjoy the freedom and the ability to adventure around the world. This type of person wants to learn about who they are through the world around them and uses adventure as a way to deepen their understanding of themselves. They tend to be highly outgoing and enjoy meeting new people and gaining new perspectives on life, as this serves their minds with a sense of adventure, too. The biggest fear of an explorer is to be trapped, experience conformity to the world around them, or endure a sense of inner emptiness. They want to live a fulfilling, authentic, unique life that teaches them plenty. The weakness of the explorer is to find themselves lost or aimless or becoming a misfit to the world around them. They may also start to run away from their fears in an effort to protect themselves. You can often find the explorer archetype working as a freelancer, blogging, and jumping between small projects as they find work wherever they go.

The Rebel

The rebel is another soul-driven type, meaning they live from their soul and a place of deep authenticity. This person believes rules were made to be broken and will frequently try to convince other people to break the rules with them. They believe in getting revenge or revolting against things and will overturn anything that isn't working, even if they are the only ones it isn't working for. They fear being powerless or ineffective at gaining their desires and use the strategies of disruption, destruction, and shock to get their way. If they are not careful, the rebel archetype can start getting into trouble with the law and engaging in crimes because they long so hard to be on the "wrong side" of things. This person will often work in careers that give them an adrenaline rush, or they will make their money under the table, so they don't have to pay "the man" for their earnings.

The Hero

The hero type is another egotistical archetype. This person always comes to the rescue of others because they get a boost to their ego when they realize they are powerful enough to be needed by others. They believe they can get through anything and will always find a way to accomplish anything that someone needs. They want to prove their worth to others through their acts of heroism and seek to master things that will improve the world for others. They are terrified of being weak, vulnerable, or scared, especially in situations where others' could witness these feelings in them. The hero archetype uses their strength and competency as a strategy and is talented with being courageous and confident. They often work as firefighters, cops, politicians, activists, non-profit organization leaders, eco-friendly CEOs, and other activist-oriented roles.

The Magician

The magician is a self-type, meaning they have a strong relationship with themselves, and they are their own driving factor. This archetype believes in their ability to make anything happen and is excellent at getting everything they want in life. Their number one goal is to understand the fundamental laws of the universe and use these laws to their ability. They also want to make dreams come true, regardless of whose dreams they might be. They are afraid of enduring unintended negative consequences from their actions, especially because they can become so fixated on getting what they want to the point they will do it at any cost. If they are not careful, the magician can be highly manipulative, and people may dread being around that person. When they learn to develop a vision and live by it, this archetype is excellent with finding win-win solutions and using their magic for everyone's benefit. They are frequently employed as inventors, planners, and researchers. Magicians also find themselves in medicine, including alternative medicine, and as charismatic leaders in new-age businesses.

The Jester

The jester is the last of the four types that are driven by their own presence. They are the humorous type and believe that you only live once, so you might as well have fun with the time you have. They love to experience the joy of every moment and live for the fulfillment of life. Their goal is to have fun and make the world a lighter, funnier place for everyone around them. They are afraid of being bored or of being boring to others, so they are always spontaneously jumping around, keeping themselves occupied, and serving humor to everyone they meet. With playing, joking, and being funny, the jester archetype can find their way through anything. They can, however, succumb to being frivolous and wasting time, which can prevent them from reaching their goals. They are often employed in positions where they can play and have fun, or they have lower positions in their careers but enjoy their work because they are constantly bringing fun into it for themselves and everyone around them. The jester archetype will often become known as the office prankster and will be admired and appreciated by most.

The Everyman

The everyman is an egotistical archetype. Their primary belief is everyone was created equally, and they desire to connect with other people. The number one goal of an everyman is to belong somewhere, and they will do anything they can to feel as though they fit in with the world around them. They are afraid of being left out or standing alone from the rest of the crowd, and they project this fear onto others, which is what drives their inclusivity. Their strategy is developing ordinary virtues and remaining down to earth, which makes them seem as though they fit in with everyone else. The everyman is at high risk of losing themselves in an effort to blend in, and they can find themselves in superficial relationships if they are not careful. They are excellent with realism, empathy, and a lack of pretense and regularly find themselves in careers that serve their community or where they get to work hard for a living.

The Lover

The lover is a soul-driven archetype that believes heavily in romance and living life with another individual. They tend to find their partner and live with that person as a significant part of their life, to the point where they may make other couples feel jealous of their great connection. The lover desires to be intimate and to experience the love and presence of another. They always want to be in a relationship and long to be surrounded by people, places, and things they love. If they cannot feel the passion for something they're doing, they don't want to be doing it. Their greatest fear is being alone or unwanted, or of finding out someone doesn't love them. They always do their best to become more physically and emotionally attractive, so people are interested in them and pay closer attention. They are passionate, grateful, appreciative, and committed. They often work jobs that fulfill their individual passions, and that allows them to bring their entire sensuality into the experience. Fashion designers, spa workers, and team-builders all tend to be the lover archetype.

The Caregiver

Caregivers are the fourth and final variety of the ego-driven archetype. They believe in loving others the same way they would love themselves and want everyone to feel their best. The caregiver feels their best when they are protecting and caring for others, and will often push themselves into caregiving positions so they can look after other people. Their number one goal is to help others, and they do so by physically taking over and doing things for other people. They fear being selfish or not being able to express adequate gratitude in their lives, and at their weakest, they can become martyrs or be exploited for their generosity. At their strongest, they are highly compassionate and generous, which helps them in their typical career paths as nurses, care aides, support workers, and assistants.

CHAPTER 16
Never Forget To Put It Together!

Independently, each piece of information you gain from analyzing a person will not say much. If you fixate on one signal, you will gain a limited understanding of why that signal is being made or what it means. You must take the time to look across a person's entire presentation to understand more about them and gain a more accurate insight into who they are and why they are expressing themselves the way they are.

At first, it may take practice to adequately put together all the cues, to the point where you reflect on experiences long after they ended. This reflection is excellent, as it allows you to give context to the many things I have taught you within this book. Eventually, you will rapidly view all the signals and put them together, in context, to create your analysis findings. You will reach this point rapidly, so don't worry about taking your time and thoroughly researching each step. Once you start observing people in action, it comes fast.

First Step: Physical Cues

The first thing you want to do is look for physical cues on a person. Before you even say hello, you have the opportunity to look at their body and gain an understanding of how they are feeling at that moment. Pay attention to their posture, where they have positioned themselves, what shared environment you are in, and what they are doing within that environment. If they happen to be moving or making gestures, pay attention to those, as well.

Whether you realize it or not, you already have an opinion of someone formulated in your subconscious mind, well before you actually talk to that person. Giving yourself an intentional moment to look at their behavior, understand their expressions, and make an opinion is an excellent way to lay the foundation of your analysis.

Once you start interacting with a person, pay attention to how their behavior is. They may remain the same, or their behavior may shift as they are now connecting with a new individual. This is a great way to rapidly gain insight into that person's baseline and who they are, so you can start to identify nuances in their behavior and deviations from their regular.

Second Step: Emotional Cues

Emotional cues can be spotted in body language, facial expressions, tone of voice, words chosen, and the overall energy of a person you are communicating with. Ideally, you want to spot the emotional cues of a person before you start talking to them or early into the conversation, so you know what to expect. Knowing someone's emotional cues means you can adjust your behavior accordingly, to be compassionate toward their emotions. If you are trying to gain something out of them, this also gives you the opportunity to create the right emotional response to have them synchronized with you and following what you are saying.

People's emotional cues can rapidly change; for example, upon seeing you, they may click into a different emotional state than they were in prior to you arriving or introducing yourself. Paying attention to these shifts helps you understand someone, the way they are feeling, and the things they are enjoying about your conversation. You can also spot what they are averse to or what they are avoiding, based on their negative emotional response factors.

Third Step: Vocal Cues

Once someone starts talking, you want to pay attention to their vocal cues. People will tell you how they are feeling in their tone of voice, expressions, word choice, pace, and the amount to which they share. Listening to someone's voice for clues to how they are feeling and what they need lets you validate any assumptions you have made until this point. They also help add more context to a person and deepen your understanding of how they feel or what they think.

Vocal cues will be most likely to deviate from baseline energy and are easiest for people to lie about, so be careful when listening to a person's voice. You might hear an energy "behind" their voice, which suggests the emotion they are conveying is not the same as the one they are genuinely feeling. These hidden emotional behaviors indicate a person is feeling insecure or is trying to hide their real feelings, which could also indicate something is potentially wrong.

Fourth Step: Baseline

Following a few minutes of observation, and interaction if it is appropriate, you must cultivate your baseline for that person. At this point, you are going to rapidly put together their physical, emotional, and verbal cues to make an assumption about what personality archetype this person is and what they are presently feeling. You will also make an assumption about what they need and what they are doing in order to fulfill that need.

Your baseline is not necessarily an accurate assumption, especially at first, so you need to be careful not to behave as though it is absolutely correct. Instead, use it as a foundation upon which to gather information and use it to either reinforce or contradict the assumptions you have made. As you continue to interact with that person, continue building out your baseline, so it is more complex and accommodates for more of their personality, such as their emotional reactions to different triggers.

Fifth Step: Deviations

After you have cultivated a baseline understanding of someone's emotions, you can start recognizing anytime they deviate away from it. Paying attention to deviations should happen only after you have a significant, confident grasp on their baseline, as this ensures you have a more accurate representation of who they are. Once you are confident in their baseline, you can start paying attention to deviations.

Deviations will show up in a person's significantly changed emotional and behavioral response to someone. If someone that has been generally calm suddenly becomes irate, for example, you know they have deviated away from their baseline. Deviations indicate how a person is feeling and, if you are trying to elicit a certain response or reaction out of them, can help you determine whether you are on the right track or not.

CHAPTER 17
Make Your Guess And Validate It

Regardless of what form of communication you are using with someone, you can guarantee that you two will never be exactly on the same page. Communication is a tricky skill, which we all interpret and experience in our own ways, making it even more challenging. Still, you must start somewhere, and the best place to start is by making a guess and then later validating it. "Guesstimating," as it is often called, means taking early cues from someone and using them to formulate an assumption of who you think a person is, how you think they behave, what they value, what they want, and how you can help them.

You will rapidly recognize that, despite how best your guesstimating is, people will always surprise you. Part of human nature is that we are all so unique that no amount of profiling can ever exactly define who we are. For that reason, people must guess and will always be both right and wrong, as they will only ever get to know the parts of us that we let them into.

Fortunately, analyzing a person to the point where you can interpret them accurately enough is all you need. You do not need to know the exact ins and outs of a person, or who they are, specifically. As long as you have an understanding of their values, desires, likes, and dislikes, and what their personality is like, you know enough.

Creating Your Original Personality Guess

Creating your original personality guess is a lot like creating your baseline understanding of a person. At this point, you want to profile them into a personality archetype so you have a clearer understanding of them. Personality archetypes are especially useful because they provide you with insight into a person's core driving factors, goals, fears, strengths, weaknesses, and potential. Understanding this information about someone means you can connect with them over things they care about and create a closer relationship with them based on this knowledge.

You can create your original personality guess by focusing on three cues: their energy, their words, and their mannerisms. Each of the 12 archetypes has a unique form of energy that determines how exuberant or outgoing they are or are not. Their words will also indicate whether they value humor, caretaking, heroism, or other such characteristics of the archetypes. Lastly, their mannerisms or how they carry themselves will provide you with something to work from, too. Look to see what topics they bring up, what types of questions they ask, and where they place their energy. The more you understand these, the easier it is for you to make accurate determinations of what a person's personality is like.

Be careful not to overthink your original personality archetype guess. Let your intuition guide you, and use your gut feeling combined with some of what you have observed from the person you are guessing for. Overthinking this initial judgment can make the entire process seemingly impossible because you fail to lay the foundation upon which you will make your official analysis. This is merely a starting point and a guiding factor in finding the true answer to which personality type each person has.

Validating Your Guess With Reinforcements

Once you have made your observation, begin to guess their archetype using reinforcements to validate your initial guess. Validation can be achieved in many ways, ranging from manipulating the situation to observing that person in different circumstances. Your overall goal is to decide whether each behavior reinforces, or contradicts, your assumption about what that person's archetype is. You might find that your initial assumption was correct, so now you gain greater context around your assumption and the true manifestation of that archetype in that individual. Or, you might find that your initial assumption was incorrect, and you were misinterpreting signals that were indicative of their true archetype. Or, perhaps, you positively interpreted symbols of their secondary archetype.

Remember that upon initially meeting someone, they will often behave differently. Even if they have no reason to, we all have an inner desire to impress others or hide from others if we are uncomfortable with that situation. The way a person presents themselves right away might not be accurate to their overall archetype but may instead be indicative of their secondary archetype. Either way, you can use their ongoing behavior to either reinforce, contradict, or clarify your assumptions about them and their behavior.

Manipulating The Situation For Validation

An excellent way to validate your assumption of someone's behavior is to observe them and the way they behave in many different situations. If you have plenty of time to spend with someone, you can let many or all of these situations occur organically through your interaction with this person. If, however, you have limited time or the circumstances you are in prevent you from fully exploring their personality, you may need to manipulate the situation.

The easiest way to manipulate the situation for validation on your initial assumption is to guide the conversation. Talk about many different things with enthusiasm, and see how the person you are communicating with responds. What topics do they bring up? What do they seem to value? What is their tonality like? Are they agreeing or disagreeing with you? Do they seem authentic in their answer, or are they saying it just to please you? All of these answers will allow you to identify whether you are accurately interpreting a situation or not.

Another way to manipulate the situation is to intentionally put yourself in specific circumstances with someone, so you can identify how they react. For example, you might intentionally take a date to your favorite restaurant, without telling them, to find out if they genuinely like the same foods you like. These types of manipulations merely manipulate the circumstances to create an opportunity for observation and should not be used to manipulate the other person. In doing so, you would lose your accurate analysis of them and have to interpret them in another way.

Looking For External Clues To Validate

External clues are an excellent way of validating your assumptions about someone and their personality. By external validations, I mean look for clues in the way they dress, the places they hang out at, who their friends are, and the way they physically interact with the world around them. Notice how they handle things, what their movements are like, and where they tend to spend most of their time.

If they are hanging out with a group of friends, are they in the center talking to everyone, or standing to the side with one or two other people, or alone entirely? At work, do they walk directly where they need to go, or do they stop and chat with people along the way? Are they a generally clean person, or do they keep their spaces messy?

This external information is a great way to validate whether you are accurate or inaccurate with your findings. The environments people spend time in, the way they carry themselves, and the methods they use for interacting with their environment and surroundings are all indicative of who they are. You can learn a lot about a person's values, preferences, and beliefs by their surroundings. Each of these perfectly works toward describing that person's personality to you, too.

Asking For Validation Outright

In some scenarios, asking for validation outright may be a perfectly acceptable way of identifying someone's personality. In doing so, you must either casually inject your questions into the conversation or ask them during times when it would be appropriate to ask such a thing.

When you are casually injecting things into a conversation, consider looking for organic ways to ask. For example, when someone tells you something about yourself, say, "Oh! You are quite outgoing, are you?" This is an excellent way to interject these questions, without directly asking someone something rather personal about themselves. Further, most people are unaware of their personality type or may be offended by it, so asking for exacting personality types is not recommended. Instead, ask questions that give you some insight into the characteristics that the person has, which allows you to profile them into an archetype on your own.

If you are in a situation where asking such questions is natural or expected in the conversation, you can always ask outright and with seriousness. For example, in an interview or on an early date with someone new, you might ask, "What would you describe your personality type as?" This may seem like a dry or overused question; however, it does get directly to the point. It is worth noting that the personality archetype that someone declares they have may not be accurate, or it may not be the personality type you see out of them. Often, people view themselves differently than others do, and people show up differently in the many relationships in their lives, which can make getting an exact representation challenging. It is wise to use this as a piece of the overall assumption you make, rather than the assumption itself. Continue to observe for clues of an accurate interpretation, and use that to help you make your dynamic view of each person.

CHAPTER 18
Be Flexible In Your Understanding

Reading body language can provide you with fairly accurate interpretations of others, though it can never give you exact interpretations. While reading body language is often accurate and gives you plenty of information to go from when it comes to communicating with others, you must understand that you can easily make mistakes while reading this form of communication. Beyond body language, facial expressions, tones, words, and even full messages can be misinterpreted by you, making your ability to fully and accurately analyze a human rather challenging.

The best thing to remember is that you do not need to be 100% accurate in order to gain enough information from body language to use it to your advantage. If you do not remain flexible in your understanding, you run the risk of holding people to inaccurate images, misinterpreting them, or even carrying lifelong opinions of them that are irrelevant to who they really are. Always be flexible in your interpretation of others', and be willing to adapt your interpretation to new information you receive. This way, you always have an accurate representation of people, which makes interacting and connecting with them far more efficient.

Your Mood May Project Onto Others

One of the most significant reasons why your analysis of another person may be incorrect is because you are projecting onto others. Projections are most likely when we make an assumption about someone else based on what we would feel, think, or do in those circumstances. If they behave as we do, we assume they are just like us. If they don't, we assume they are just like someone that we know that they *are* similar to. You might use this information to unfairly judge someone or categorize them based on how another person is, and not they themselves.

Even if you are not generally the type to project onto others, you might find yourself projecting based on a mood you are in or the way you are feeling. These temporary emotional states can lead to our perspective of the world around us, shifting, which can impact our ability to analyze others. Always be sure to check yourself and your mood before analyzing others to ensure you remain objective in your observations. If you find you cannot reasonably tell the difference, avoid trying to analyze anyone as you might create unfair first interpretations, which can be challenging to revise at a later date.

Your Judgment May Be Clouded

Your judgment can easily become clouded by other people and unusual circumstances if you are not careful. Clouded judgment can lead to you making false or unfair assumptions about people or possibly misinterpreting them altogether because you failed to remain objective in your observation. The most common reason to have clouded judgment is that you made an assumption about a person before you had enough information to do so. If you find yourself in the habit of feeling as though you already know someone before you have even talked to them, you are robbing yourself of the opportunity to actually know and understand other people. You must communicate with someone and interact with them first before making your assumption; otherwise, you will lack essential information for your analysis.

The most likely ways to prejudge someone include judging them by their looks, listening to gossip or rumors that were being spread about them, or judging them based on the way they behaved in one isolated incident. If you have made a judgment about anyone based on this information, it is worth it to revisit your judgment and consider that it may be inaccurate. With an open mind, review your assumption and look for new evidence to validate or contradict it without leaning into cognitive bias.

That Person May Be Behaving Differently

One especially important reason to remain flexible when gauging people's personalities is that they may be behaving differently than they normally would, which would interrupt your ability to accurately judge them. If you meet or are interacting with someone during a time when they are behaving differently than how they normally would, you will not get to know who they really are. If you do not already know someone and they behave in a way that is off-putting, it may be worthwhile to assume this was just a mood they were in and to give them a second chance. If, after that second chance, they continue to behave the same way, then you can assume this is their personality.

One small factor you can look at that might indicate an overall personality trait, rather than a mood-related behavior, is how they seem to act about things unrelated to the topic they are reacting to. For example, let's say a customer comes into your store behaving erratically because they are angry with something they have experienced. If their spouse called and they had to answer, listening to the way they addressed their partner while angry would be a great way to determine if they were more aggressive overall or if their anger was isolated to the present experience. This same approach can be applied to any number of situations to determine someone's likely overall personality on occasions where you do not have a lot of time to get to know it otherwise.

You May Have Misinterpreted Your Gut

Your gut feeling about a person will virtually always be right, but you may have misinterpreted the messages your gut was giving you. People often misinterpret these messages when they find themselves in circumstances that feel too familiar, especially if it is a negative familiar. For example, if you have a trauma or a bad memory from a specific circumstance, you might misinterpret people or their behaviors when you are with them in a similar circumstance because you have emotional flashbacks. These emotional flashbacks can be strong enough to prevent you from accurately interpreting other people because you are viewing them through a heavily biased lens.

It is important to remember that, despite the similarities that exist between people and circumstances throughout our lives, no two people are the same; therefore, the experiences you have with different people will always turn out differently. If you find yourself experiencing emotional triggers and misinterpreting signals someone is giving you, assume that your gut instinct is being falsely interpreted, or triggered, and look for other clues to learn more about that person. Otherwise, do not overthink your gut, and trust what it has to say.

You May Have Over Thought It

Overthinking can sabotage many things, including your ability to analyze people. Your initial analysis of someone will include recent judgments based on their actions, words, behaviors, and other cues you picked up on during your communications. At the time of you making these assumptions, your answers were most likely to be accurate. The trouble with overthinking things is that, while doing it, you genuinely believe you are not overthinking something; rather, you are "realizing after the fact" that you likely interpreted it wrong. This is rooted in insecurity, not a genuine change of heart in your gut feeling. Be wary of this behavior.

There is one reliable way to determine if you are overthinking something or if you genuinely misjudged something. If you are agonizing over something and playing it over and over in your mind, trying to determine if you accurately interpreted something, you are overthinking it. You repetitively recalling the event will actually change your memory of the event, therefore giving you an inaccurate interpretation of it. Never change your mind once you have made it up *unless* you gain reliable new information that is worth changing your mind over. For example, if you meet with that person again and their new behavior contradicts your initial interpretation, now it is worth it to re-analyze and reconsider your initial assumption. Otherwise, you are likely overthinking it!

CONCLUSION

Congratulations on completing *How To Analyze People!*
Knowing how to accurately analyze people is an imperative part of anyone's life. From everyday communication to conducting business dealings or meeting new people, knowing how to analyze other people is a significantly useful life skill. Through your accurate ability to analyze people, you gain the ability to recognize their characteristics, understand their personality, identify their likes and dislikes, and connect with them in a way that feels good to them.

As you continue to practice analyzing people, you will discover that your understanding of different cues and signs grows. Seeing different behaviors in the flesh provides a level of context that cannot be gained in reading, as you are able to interpret these signals through the tangible senses of your body. Continue analyzing people in as many situations as possible to refine your interpretation of these signals, as this will allow you to deepen your innate knowledge of people and conduct more accurate analysis.

When it comes to using your analysis, you must remember to always use it for the genuine good of everyone. Use it to better understand people, connect with them in a more positive way, and support them throughout their life. Never feel as though you have to manipulate other people, even if you think those manipulations will create more positive in their lives. You are not obligated to people-please, nor are you obligated to use this information to take better care of others. On the contrary, you should use this information to help you relate better with people while connecting with them on an individual level in a more meaningful way.

If you have chosen to explore human analysis for a unique purpose, it is best to practice using it in that area of your life as often as you can. The more you use it in this area of your life, the better you will be at interpreting signs and using them to your desired advantage. Know, too, that what you learn in this area of your life will serve in other areas, as once you know how to interpret body language in one way, it becomes a lot easier to do it in other ways, as well.

The next step you should take after reading this book is to begin getting serious about analyzing others but also learning to analyze yourself. Whenever you can, get into observation mode and observe what your natural interactions are like. Your interactions will naturally shift as you are now paying such close attention to them; however, you will still get the opportunity to see how you generally behave, or what feels natural for you. Observing your own behavior is excellent because it gives you the opportunity to express yourself more intentionally around others, thus creating the image you desire to create with them. Further, it gives you the opportunity to understand yourself better and help yourself grow in whatever direction you desire.

Whether you were here for a reason, or you were here to simply learn more about people and the world around you, I want to thank you for reading *How To Analyze People*. I hope you learned plenty about human analysis and are feeling confident in your ability to interpret and understand people as you need to.

Before you go, I ask that you please take a moment to honestly review *How To Analyze People* on Amazon. Your feedback would be greatly appreciated, as it allows others to discover this title and use it to support their own understanding of people. Further, it allows me to understand how you enjoyed this title, so I can create more great content for you!

Thank you, and best of luck with analyzing people. Remember, trust your gut, and stay flexible! You might be surprised to discover what you learn about people, the more open you remain.

DESCRIPTION

Human analysis is a natural part of our everyday lives, yet very few people genuinely understand what it is or know how to consciously read the cues other people are giving them. If you find yourself constantly overthinking people's behaviors, analyzing people's voices, and feeling insecure or uncertain around their cues, you need to learn more about human analysis.

The process of analyzing people is relevant to countless areas of your life. From a primal and biological perspective, human analysis enables you to feel confident that you are not surrounded by someone that is dangerous, or who could become dangerous at any point in the future. In more modern ways, human analysis can help you trust people, make sales, get to know your date, connect with friends and family, feel more confident around people, enjoy healthier connections with others, or even get to know yourself better.

Despite the fact that your subconscious brain already knows how to analyze people, your conscious brain may have no idea. By reading *How To Analyze People,* you will uncover excellent strategies for bringing your conscious awareness on board with analyzing people, so you feel more confident in your interpretations. Further, you can use this information strategically to improve your ability to connect with or work with others. This book provides you with excellent, in-depth guidance for analyzing people, leaving no questions unanswered. You will discover countless techniques that allow you to make quick, efficient, and meaningful assumptions, and to validate those assumptions, so your findings are accurate.

Some of the specific topics we cover in *How To Analyze People* include:

- Why you should analyze people and the various methods for getting started
- The importance of body language and how to read someone's body
- Facial expressions and the necessary steps for reading micro-expressions
- What someone's eyes say about them, and how to interpret eye movement like an FBI agent
- How your intuition plays into reading people and analyzing their behaviors
- What emotional energy is and how to read it on people
- How to identify someone's baseline and observe their deviations (and why)
- The meaning of phrases like cluster gestures and mirrored behavior, and why it matters to you
- How to put the reading together, make an educated guess, and validate it

- The importance of staying flexible to learn as much as possible
- And more!

By following the step-by-step guide for reading someone's behavior that is detailed within this book, and including the many additional nuances we discuss, you will discover exactly how to accurately analyze people. Understand that it will take practice on your behalf to put context to what you are taught, but with this book, you can read anyone with ease and confidence.

Discover how to stop overthinking and overanalyzing, and start clearly understanding people today! Purchase *How To Analyze People* and uncover the unique, hidden languages of humankind, and how these languages can be used to communicate both consciously and subconsciously with other people. You won't be disappointed that you did!

www.ingramcontent.com/pod-product-compliance
Lightning Source LLC
Chambersburg PA
CBHW071509070526
44578CB00001B/489